Nuclear War, Deterrence
and
Morality

William V. O'Brien

NUCLEAR WAR DETERRENCE and MORALITY

NEWMAN PRESS

Westminster   New York   Glen Rock
Amsterdam   Toronto

NIHIL OBSTAT: Rev. John F. Cronin, S.S.
Censor Deputatus

IMPRIMATUR: ✠ Patrick A. O'Boyle
Archbishop of Washington

January 13, 1967

The Nihil Obstat and Imprimatur are official declarations that a book or pamphlet is free of doctrinal or moral error. No implication is contained therein that those who have granted the Nihil Obstat and Imprimatur agree with the contents, opinions or statements expressed.

Library of Congress
Catalog Card Number: 67-15720

Published by Newman Press
Editorial Office: 304 W. 58th St., N. Y., N. Y. 10019
Business Office: Westminster, Md. 21157

Manufactured in the
United States of America

Contents

vi   *Contents*

Preface

The purpose of this book is to call attention to the major problems involved in defining and applying the moral limits of modern war and deterrence. Such an undertaking necessarily exposes the writer to a crossfire of criticism. Some say that war cannot be limited. The only thing to be said about it today is that it is immoral. Others say that higher values — *e.g.,* justice, freedom, religion — must be defended, if necessary by war. Restraints on "just" wars are viewed as inadmissible interference with the defense of these higher rights. Thus, to extreme proponents of each view those who are concerned with the problems of limiting war are against both "peace" and "justice."

It is the contention of this book that part of the task of working for peace with justice is to delineate the moral limits of war. For wars continue to occur despite increasingly serious efforts to prevent them. This book also takes the position that no "higher cause" justifies unlimited war. The price for continued justification of some defensive wars is a markedly greater effort at limitation both of the occasions of recourse to force and the means employed once such recourse is deemed morally permissible.

However, it is not the opposition of extreme and simplistic advocates of peace and justice that presents the greatest obstacle to efforts to delineate the morally permissible limits of war and deterrence. The real obstacle is the vacuum of authoritative analysis and informed public opinion regarding the issues of morality in the nuclear age. No one has wanted to look into the eye of the humanly unbearable hurricane which is modern war and deterrence. The moralists have avoided a real confrontation with the subject and the average citizen has not complained about the absence of adequate moral guidance on it. He is no more anxious than the moralists to come to grips with such frightening and difficult problems. But time is running out both for the moralists and for the average citizen. We are all caught up in a race to escape what Vatican II described as a "terrible trap."

In this book I have addressed myself to that part of the task of "working for peace" which is concerned with the limitation of war. I have sought to avoid pious pleas for sweeping solutions to difficult problems. On the other hand, I have tried to show the tensions and conflicts that presently exist between the moral principles that the Church has laid down and the policies of modern states with respect to war and deterrence. In so doing I have questioned the authority, relevance and adequacy of some of the moral principles. I have also questioned the defense policies of the United States and other states.

This book, then, undertakes to summarize and analyze the state of the question with regard to nuclear war, deterrence and morality today. Since the state of the question is far from satisfactory it is the hope of the author that progress — both on the practical issues of war and deterrence and within the empirical and normative disciplines that may enable us to define and judge "progress" in these matters — will soon make this book obsolete.

In preparing this book I sought the advice and criticism of a number of people. I should like to thank them here for their generous and valuable help. My thanks go to: Reverend Robert Bosc, S.J., *Action Populaire,* Paris; Dr. Donald Brandon, Department of Political Science, University of San Francisco; Dr. James Dougherty, University of Pennsylvania, St. Joseph's College; Dr. Victor C. Ferkiss, Department of Government, Georgetown University; Mr. James Finn, *Worldview;* Mr. Harry Flannery, AFL-CIO; Dr. Richard Hartigan, Department of Political Science, Loyola of Chicago; Dr. Charles Herzfeld, Advanced Research Projects Agency, Department of Defense; Msgr. George G. Higgins, Social Action Department, United States Catholic Conference; Rev. Brian A. McGrath, S.J., Administrative Vice-President, Georgetown University; Reverend Robert Mohan, Catholic University; Reverend John Courtney Murray, S.J., Woodstock College; Reverend John M. Paul, St. Paul's College; Dr. Paul Ramsey, Department of Religion, Princeton; Mr. Peter F. Steinfels, *Commonweal;* Dr. Robert W. Tucker, The Johns Hopkins University; Dr. Theodore Weber, Candler School of Theology, Emory University.

1

War and Morality
in an Age of Conflict

Conflict, international and domestic, has characterized all ages. But our own time has seen such widespread, intense, deep-rooted conflicts that it has been called an age of conflict. No analysis of contemporary moral problems of war and peace can be helpful unless it recognizes this salient feature of the world in which we live. A realistic analysis of our time must begin with a recognition that most modern conflicts arise out of deep-rooted religious, ideological, social, and racial differences. In this respect our age differs from others in the period since the Thirty Years' War ended in 1648, in which widespread and intense conflict resulted more from greed and lust for power than from the pursuit of profound ideological goals.

The nature of contemporary conflict is evidenced by the 20th century concept of total war wherein all the resources and fundamental values of one society are engaged in a life-or-death struggle with those of another. To lose decisively in such a conflict could mean the loss of the right of the defeated society to live in accordance with its fundamental values, and could jeopardize the integrity of each individual's freedom of conscience.

This is also an age in which the ways man can destroy his enemies and himself have reached fantastic development. So destructive are some of our weapons that it would be suicidal or grossly counterproductive ever to use them. But the seemingly inevitable conflicts produced by the ideological mainsprings of our age make recourse to these dreaded weapons a constant possibility. The incendiary dangers of international conflict threaten to trap antagonists in the iron grip of weapons systems that develop their own logic and necessities. Such systems may wrest the decisions of war and peace from the very hands of those who created them.

The reaction of enlightened statesmen and citizens to this predicament has been to erect legal and moral barriers against recourse to armed force as an instrument of foreign policy, and to seek to eliminate or control the more dangerous means of war by prohibiting their use or by physically dismantling them. These efforts may be viewed in two ways. If one is grimly realistic, they can be scorned as too little and too late to be effective. Conflict persists, wars break out, the arms race, or — more accurately — a number of arms races spiral upward. This state of affairs is the "given" in our problem of relating morality to modern war.

On the other hand, it may be argued that we have made some progress. It was only a half century ago that serious statesmen, military theorists and intellectuals were defending the ennobling effects of war as a social institution. At that time, war was still a legal instrument of foreign policy. Today there is a wide consensus in support of international law prohibiting recourse to aggressive war. The practical problems are more in the realm of interpretation and enforcement than of principles. Evidence that mankind abhors total war, whether conventional or nuclear, lies in the fact that most post-World War II conflict has not taken that extreme form.

Whether previous efforts to limit war and its more extreme means strike us as being pitifully inadequate or as evidence of modest human progress, our present "dangerous" world (as Secretary Rusk calls it) urgently requires renewed efforts on behalf of international peace, law and order.

What is the role of Catholics in pressing these efforts? In particular, what have Catholics to say about the dilemma created by the threat of nuclear war, in an age of conflict in which the chances of war occurring are high?

The influence of Catholics has not been conspicuous in efforts to control war during the period that begins roughly with the Hague Peace Conference of 1899. Rather, the principal inspiration of this period has come from the secular humanism which triumphed over competing philosophical viewpoints in the 19th century. The popes and the hierarchy, as well as Catholic scholars like John Eppstein, Jacques Maritain, and Heinrich Rommen contributed to thought and action on behalf of world peace, law and order, but even in nominally Catholic countries their influence was limited compared to that of the sociopolitical and intellectual "establishments".

Whatever the validity of this view, recent years have witnessed a striking rise in the prestige of the Catholic Church, its popes, its intellectual and moral leaders and the political influence exercised by statesmen and citizens in many key countries. Catholic intellectuals today should not grumble in their ghettos against the non-Catholic *élite* who scorn their views.

Today a substantial part of the world looks to the Catholic Church for guidance in facing the moral dilemmas of our time. What have the Church and Catholic tradition to say about these dilemmas? It is the purpose of this book to assess the teaching of the Catholic Church on war generally and on nuclear war and deterrence in particular. When this has been done, the implications of this assessment will be applied to those responsible for making the Catholic contribution to efforts to limit war.

Two Reactions to the Challenge

Few Catholics have been willing or able to develop positions on the morality of nuclear war based on the teachings of the Church. Nor has the Church been overwhelmed with demands from the faithful for clearer guidance on this subject. However, among the comparative minority of clergy and laymen who have taken a position, there have been two sharply distinguishable Catholic reactions. On the one hand, some have attempted to analyze the problems in terms of traditional "just war" doctrines. At the same time, however, there has been a resurgence of Catholic pacifism that contrasts dramatically with predominant Catholic reactions to recent wars. Many of these pacifists urge unilateral disarmament, regardless of the threats posed by the ideological conflicts we have mentioned. The fact that proponents of various pacifist positions include Catholics of stature, integrity and intellectual accomplishment underscores the extent to which the age of conflict and of total war challenges traditional Catholic views on morally permissible, just wars.

Clearly the problem is most serious for American Catholics. There are Catholics in such countries as Great Britain and France that possess nuclear weapons. There are Catholics in other nations that cooperate in plans for use of nuclear weapons without possessing them independently. There are Catholics in countries whose security is based in some measure on the American nuclear deterrent. But the greatest nuclear power and the cornerstone for the defense of the non-Communist world is the United States. American Catholics are confronted with the necessity of reconciling the demands of their faith with the necessities of defense, or of reaching a moral judgment that such reconciliation cannot be accomplished and of acting accordingly.

This book will undertake to examine our overall practical and moral predicament. Having framed the issues, it will review the teaching of the Church about war in general. It will trace the reactions of the hierarchy, of Catholic moralists, and of qualified scholars to the problems of modern war and morality. Catholic teaching will then be applied to the specific problems that keep men working late in the White House, the Pentagon, the Department of State, the headquarters of the Strategic Air Command and the Arms Control and Disarmament Agency. We hope to identify the central issues and the practical responsibilities raised by nuclear war and deterrence in an age of conflict. These issues and responsibilities concern not only popes, bishops, moral theologians, statesmen, generals, and scientists but all of us who have been given some degree of intellectual and moral awareness of this great problem.

The writer starts from a modified just war point of view. The pacifist case is not presented except as necessary in re-examining the just war tradition in the light of the new problems of total conventional and nuclear war. It can be stated as a fact that at least since the time of St. Augustine the official teaching of the Church has permitted just war and repeatedly rejected pacifism.

This remains the case after Vatican Council II. We do not suggest that a strong case for pacifism and particularly for nuclear pacifism is not conceivable; the majority both within the hierarchy and the laity may be wrong and the pacifist minority right. The reader will find references in the bibliography to pacifist works which he may wish to consult.

The starting point of this book is as follows: The Church has traditionally admitted the right of political societies to defend themselves and, in some cases, to use force offensively for grave causes. Nuclear war compels us to question the continued relevance of the traditional teaching which was based on factual assumptions with respect to weaponry that are vastly removed from our present problems. We shall attempt to see whether the traditional rights of recourse to force have survived the appearance of nuclear weapons and if so, in what form.

The Ascending Totality of Total War

Historically, our present predicament begins with the concept of total war. A total war is one in which an entire society wages war on another society. The essential characteristics of the enemy society are a target upon which all available means are unleashed. The enemy society's way of life is the potential victim of total victory. Total war, unlike most wars of the modern era (since the emergence of nation-states in the 16th and 17th centuries) is not a war in which armed forces are deputized like athletes to decide controverted issues in arenas largely removed from the political, social and economic lives of the warring countries. Rather it is a war in which every aspect of the enemy's life is an object of attack in one form or another, *e.g.*, if not military, certainly psychological, economic, subversive or other non-military. In such a conflict there is a clearly discernible tendency for the parties to be blinded by the stakes at issue and to adopt, often explicitly, the attitude that the end justifies the means. This attitude is often fortified by fear and desperation if defeat appears imminent. Since a total war involves a clash of fundamental values, the belief that "our side" is "right" and the enemy "wrong" results in serious relaxation of moral restraint insofar as the conduct of the conflict is concerned.

Although there are evidences of the total war mentality in the wars growing out of the French Revolution and in the American Civil War, the concept of total war in its modern sense had its first major trial run in World War I. Technological advances had made total war a practical possibility, whereas this was not the case in earlier conflicts.

But the utter depravity of World War I turned men's stomachs and disposed their minds and hearts to oppose any repetition of what they conceived as a vast and obscene "swindle" and slaughter. In the twenties and early thirties it was hard to imagine another war like the "Great War" of 1914-1918. It took the particularly vicious nature of Nazi and other totalitarian tyranny and aggression to arouse, in World War II, a renewed willingness to fight and an attitude demanding "unconditional surrender", supported by a willingness to condone all means, no matter how terrible, that promised success. True, a few voices like that of Father John Ford protested fire-bomb raids on whole cities, even in the context of a war to defeat the monstrous Axis empire.* But such voices were few and unheeded. It is now clear that we were laying the basis in World War II for a major part of our present moral dilemma. In World War II the United States seems to have accepted the proposition that *all* means are permissible in total conflict with a truly evil enemy. This may turn out to be the most tragic of the many bitter legacies left us by the Axis powers — an adversary so patently evil that the habit of unlimited response to evil was inordinately encouraged.

Thus by the time the United States destroyed Hiroshima and Nagasaki with atomic bombs there was a tendency to argue that these attacks were justified since they were simply more efficient ways of doing what was already accepted as normal in aerial warfare. The Japanese "war effort" and will to fight was being attacked by atomic bombs just as it had been by fire-bomb raids. The argument that hundreds of thousands of Americans who might have been lost in assaults on the Japanese homeland were

* John C. Ford, S.J., "The Morality of Obliteration Bombing," in 5 *Theological Studies* (September, 1944), pp. 261-309.

saved was a major justification. It was also said that a speedy defeat was better for the Japanese than a prolonged and hopeless resistance to overwhelming American power. Few noticed that the latter argument was repeatedly criticized by Americans and others when advanced by sincere Prussian military commanders and military scientists before World War I as partial justification for the proposition that in war necessity knows no law. Thus, a particularly galling aspect of our present nuclear dilemma is that we have built our attitudes on World War II "city-busting" precedents which ought to have been sharply challenged when they were made. They were not challenged, in part because of the hypnotic influence of the Axis tyranny and the danger it raised for the world.

Still the mentality of total war did not completely pervade the post-World War II epoch, even after the lines of the Cold War had hardened. The United States worked for the success of the UN, advanced the Baruch Plan and grappled with the problems of removing atomic power from national to international control. The hostility of the Communist bloc and the adamant insistence of the Communists on alternative disarmament arrangements, which only the most naive could seriously consider, insured the failure of the world's first efforts at nuclear disarmament. Instead, the United States and the Soviet Union raced on to replace the "absolute weapon" of early atomic days with the H-bomb which dwarfed the dreaded "bomb" of Hiroshima.

2

The Nuclear Arsenal

What kind of weapon is an H-bomb and how does it differ from smaller nuclear weapons? The Hiroshima A-bomb was in the 20 kiloton class, *i.e.,* its explosive power equalled 20,000 tons of TNT. Its blast and heat effects substantially destroyed Hiroshima. More specifically:

> Official statistics on the destruction and death caused by the bomb were released by Japan six months after the war: 4.7 square miles of Hiroshima were destroyed; 40,653 dwellings (81.1 percent of the total) were destroyed; 8,396 severely damaged; and 1,111 slightly damaged. No buildings entirely escaped damage. Of the human casualties, 71,379 were killed or missing; 68,023 were injured — 19,691 of them seriously hurt. The United States Strategic Bomb Survey was less precise, estimating the dead at between 70,000 and 80,000 with similar figures for the injured. Compared to the single fire-bomb raid on Tokyo of March 9/10, the atomic bomb wounded more but killed less. In Tokyo, a city with a population density of 103,000 per square mile inside the area bombed as compared to 35,000 in Hiroshima, the fire-bomb raid killed 83,793 and wounded 40,918. [Len Giovannitti and Fred Freed, *The Decision to Drop the Bomb* (New York: Coward-McCann, 1965), p. 269.]

Radioactive fallout from the explosion caused many deaths and illnesses among the survivors.

However, the fall-out from an A-bomb in the kiloton class is "local" and "temporary." With the later development of nuclear devices in the 1-2 kiloton class, so-called tactical nuclear weapons, it became possible to use nuclear weapons with explosive power that is tremendously superior to that of existing conventional

8

weapons but has comparatively little danger of extensive fall-out contamination beyond the immediate area of impact. While contamination is still a grave danger to those in the area of impact, the danger apparently does not persist very long. Thus it would appear that the main moral problem posed by kiloton nuclear weapons is the capacity of the larger ones (*e.g.,* 20 kilotons) to "take out" all or a considerable portion of a large city without any possibility of discriminating between combatants and noncombatants, or military and non-military targets. Even the so-called small, clean kiloton devices may be quite indiscriminate if used in heavily populated areas. The question of fall-out and its many short-range and long-range effects is also raised but it is not nearly as vital as the question of indiscriminate destruction.

When we turn to the megaton, *i.e.,* devices measured in millions of tons of TNT, we confront an increase in destructive power so great that some consider them different in kind from the kiloton weapons. The blast effects and heat of a hydrogen bomb would virtually destroy a city like New York. Moreover, H-bombs produce radioactive fall-out that poisons humans and animals, the earth, plant life, man-made objects, over very large areas and for long periods of time. Much depends upon weather and geographic factors. An H-bomb dropped on Washington, D.C. might inflict serious damage throughout a wide swath of territory from Norfolk, Virginia to Harrisburg, Pennsylvania. The H-bomb detonated by the U.S. in the Marshall Islands on March 1, 1954 was capable of blanketing an area of 7,000 square miles with radioactive fall-out. Particularly if the explosion is a "ground burst", *i.e.,* exploded on or close to the earth so that it draws up great quantities of contaminated earth and distributes it throughout the atmosphere, fall-out may become global. It will continue for years to fall back on the earth on enemies, friends, neutrals, even on those who exploded the device that caused the contamination.

Such fall-out causes genetic mutations, bone cancer and other maladies that threaten future generations as well as the earth's present inhabitants. After more than twenty years we still know little about the evil consequences of fall-out from comparatively infrequent nuclear tests, much less what they would be after a major nuclear exchange. A clear indication of the grave dangers of nuclear testing is the fact that on August 5, 1963 the United States, the United Kingdom and the Soviet Union, which depend on nuclear power to maintain the "balance of terror" and their position as great powers, agreed to a ban on testing in the atmosphere. They overrode the demands by some military men and scientists in their countries to retain freedom to develop better nuclear weapons.

However, the worldwide fall-out threat is thought by experts to be the least of the dangers of nuclear weapons. It is the probable "local" fall-out within a nation attacked with hundreds of nuclear devices that is most dreadful to contemplate. In testimony regarding the 1966 military budget, Secretary of Defense McNamara stated before the subcommittee of the House of Representatives, March 2, 1965:

> The strategic objectives of our general nuclear war forces are:
> 1. To deter a deliberate nuclear attack upon the United States and its allies by maintaining a clear and convincing capability to inflict unacceptable damage on an attacker, even were that attacker to strike first.
> 2. In the event such a war should nevertheless occur, to limit damage to our population and industrial capacities.
> The first of these capabilities (required to deter potential aggressors) we call assured destruction, *i.e.,* the capability to destroy the aggressor as a viable society, even after a well-planned and executed surprise attack on our forces. The second capability we call damage limitation, *i.e.,* the capability to reduce the weight of the enemy attack by both offensive and defensive measures and to provide a degree of protection for the population against the effects of nuclear detonations. . . .
> Based on the projected threat for the early 1970's and the most likely planning factors for that time period, our calculations show that even after absorbing a first strike, our already authorized strategic missile force, if it were directed against the aggressor's urban areas, could cause more than 100 million fatalities and destroy about 80 per cent of his industrial capacity. If our manned bombers were then to mount a follow-on attack against urban areas, fatalities would be increased by 10 to 15 million and industrial destruction another percent or two. [U.S. House of Representatives,

Subcommittee on Department of Defense Appropriations, *Hearings,* pt. 3. 89th Cong., 1st Sess. (Washington: Government Printing Office, 1965), pp. 34, 40.]

When Mr. McNamara turned to the problems of "damage limiting" defensive measures by the United States, he indicated the magnitude of losses in a nuclear war in the following estimate of the probable consequences of spending more money on constructing fall-out shelters and other damage-limiting measures:

ESTIMATED EFFECT ON U.S. FATALITIES OF
ADDITIONS TO THE APPROVED DAMAGE LIMITING
PROGRAM (BASED ON 1970 POPULATION
OF 210,000,000)

Additional Investment	Millions of U.S. Fatalities	
	Early urban attack	Delayed urban attack
$0	149	122
$5,000,000,000	120	90
$15,000,000,000	96	59
$25,000,000,000	78	41

(U.S. House of Representatives, *Hearings,* p. 41.)

We should keep these estimates in mind as we analyze the moral issues raised by the age of international conflict and nuclear war and deterrence. It is pointless to talk about "the A-bomb" or "the H-bomb"; moreover, it is not particularly useful to belabor the point that there are many conceivable situations in which some nuclear weapons could be used without violating any norms of the just war or other theories permitting use of armed force. Thus, it is reasonably clear that destruction of an enemy naval vessel off Antarctica with a 1-kiloton device, judged in a vacuum without reference to anything else, would appear to be morally defensible. But this is far from the heart of our problem.

We should, rather, think in terms of "weapons systems" which include thousands of nuclear warheads and thousands of means of delivery including manned bombers, missiles ranging from short-range to those which may be fired from one continent against another at distances from 5,000 to 9,000 miles or more. These weapons systems are controlled by extremely complex, highly automated command and communications systems, supported by far-reaching administrative and logistical machinery. These systems in turn depend on an endless research and development effort which creates, improves and replaces them.

The implications of these elaborate war-deterring and war-making structures cut in many directions. One common reaction of morally concerned people, including recent popes, is that the dehumanization of the system reduces human control to a dangerous extent. On the other hand, we should not ignore the heavy emphasis on communication and control features designed to maximize human control of weapons systems which has been characteristic of the Kennedy-Johnson-McNamara defense policies.

The moral problems of nuclear war and deterrence go back to the drawing boards on which modern weapons systems are drafted. They also go back to the decisions of Administrations about defense policies and to reactions to those decisions by Congress and the voters. Thus political acceptance of "more bang for the buck" policies of massive retaliation implied heavy moral responsibility for the existence of weapons systems based on those concepts.

It is misleading to focus discussions of the morality of nuclear war and deterrence solely or even primarily on the legitimacy of a particular President giving an order or of an air force general pushing a button. There are grave moral problems for such individuals, but if the button-pushing stage is ever reached there will presumably be very little "choice" left. The "system" will have operated as it was structured to operate, given the occurrence of various contingencies. For the individual President or officer the moral issues originate at the moment when he agrees to serve in a capacity that could require his performance of the fateful acts. For the rest of us, the moral issues go back through the years during which "the system" was being established.

The Balance of Terror

Today we enjoy a degree of peace and order insofar as direct military confrontations between the nuclear super-powers are concerned. But that peace rests on the "balance of terror." The balance of terror is the situation in which the principal nuclear antagonists, the United States and the Soviet Union, both have the capacity substantially to destroy the other's society (as we have seen in the testimony of Secretary McNamara). The survivors of even a short nuclear war would inherit a world of desolation, contamination, sickness, hunger, poverty, and extremely grave social-psychological problems. The "winner" would have the dubious privilege of visiting and perhaps of attempting to "rule" the "defeated" in their ruins. Such a war obviously cannot lead to "victory." It makes no sense for powers seeking material gain or ideological supremacy to destroy the very objects of their ambitions.

Both sides know that general nuclear war would be self-defeating. Their leaders have said so repeatedly. But if one side has such power to destroy the other, the latter cannot fail to seek equal or superior means. Both the United States and its allies and the Soviet Union and its allies believe that the other side would overturn their basic social system if it were able to do so. Cherishing the values of these basic social systems, each side feels obliged to deter conquest by the threat of nuclear war.

Nor is deterrence of major attack the only use of these terrible weapons. Nuclear weapons have numerous "uses" even when they are not used. Nuclear "brinkmanship", a term coined, perhaps unfortunately, by Secretary of State Dulles, is a game that sometimes tempts the international politician. Khrushchev's implied threats against British and French cities in the 1956 Suez crisis, and speculation about the use of American nuclear weapons against the Chinese Communists or North Vietnam come to mind. Even as a deterrent, nuclear weapons have proved invaluable since they deter non-nuclear as well as nuclear attacks. A would-be aggressor can never be sure that his non-nuclear attack may not be met with a nuclear response.

Ambiguity about intent is thus joined with the hope of those who develop nuclear weapons systems that their actual use is unlikely. Such systems are maintained to insure insofar as possible that they will not be used. The day nuclear weapons are used is the day they have failed to produce the deterrent effect for which they were made.

Maintenance of the balance of terror is difficult and hazardous. The "stability" of the relationship between the great nuclear powers becomes all-important. De-stabilizing developments are viewed with dismay, sometimes even when they may mean an improvement in one's own position. For example, it is not in the interest of the United States to gain a de-stabilizing advantage over the Soviet Union if that development seems likely to panic the Soviets and induce precipitate actions. Such actions might lead to the very war which the nuclear deterrent is supposed to prevent. The world of the balance of terror is one of paradoxes wherein avowed enemies try to educate and help each other with respect to the essential components of the balance of terror while continuing their competitive co-existence under the umbrella of their deterrent forces. Thus, novelist Eugene Burdick was not being entirely fanciful when he depicted a situation wherein an American President was obliged to order the U.S. Air Force to destroy New York to prove his good faith and honest regret with respect to the "accidental" destruction of Moscow due to a breakdown of the "fail-safe" system.*

* Eugene Burdick and Harvey Wheeler, *Fail Safe* (New York: McGraw-Hill, 1962): The Strategic Air Command's "Fail-Safe" system to prevent accidental triggering of nuclear war apparently requires United States bombers to turn back about two hours flying time this side of Russia.

The United States — which denied Soviet charges that SAC bombers were endangering peace by sorties close to Russian territory — has not disclosed details of the safeguard procedure.

But the approximate location of the line beyond which no bomber would pass except on direct orders from the President was indicated in testimony before a House Appropriations subcommittee.

Lt. General C.S. Irvine, Air Force Chief of Staff for Material, testifying about the use of missiles and manned bombers, said:

"You can start bombers toward the target and call them back. This is part of the SAC philosophy. You can have a fleet of airplanes as far as Ireland and unless they receive the 'go ahead' they could turn around and come back."

[Then] Secretary of Defense Neil H. McElroy and Gen. Nathan F. Twining, Chairman of the Joint Chiefs of Staff, told newsmen that a foolproof method existed for calling bombers home even though they may

It should be emphasized that the balance of terror is more than a mere marshalling of weapons and delivery systems. It rests on mutual expectations on the part of the nuclear powers concerning attitudes and behavior with respect to nuclear war. The key concept is that of "credibility" of the threat to execute a nuclear attack under certain circumstances. This is a crucial point at which morality enters into the discussion of nuclear war and deterrence.

The Political-Military Situation in Which the Morality of War is Debated

In summary we may identify the following political-military facts confronting the world as we debate the morality of modern means of war and deterrence.

(1) Conflict continues and may be expected to pervade great areas of the world. It is debatable whether the actual manifestations of Communist-anti-Communist conflict will reflect the fundamental collision of values and aspirations of the antagonists. Already we have seen the emergence of different, competing Communist states, blocs, and international revolutionary and evolutionary political parties and movements. Optimism over the prospects of lessened conflict of the kind that can produce hot wars must be cautious. As more intense hatreds and suspicions seem to lessen between some Communists and non-Communists,

---

have left American bases bound toward the "Fail-Safe" line in response to an alert. Elton C. Fray, "U.S. Bombers Turn Back Two Hours From Russia," in *Washington Post and Times Herald,* April 28, 1958.

Should there be a real alert based on a warning of possible attack, the force would be launched under positive control which makes certain that no SAC airplane can pass beyond proper bounds far from the Soviet Union or its satellites without additional unequivocal orders which can come only from the President of the U.S. These procedures have been established as defensive measures for the security of the U.S. and the free world and have been designed to insure the invulnerability of forces which will strike only in the event of aggression. "Guidance Statement on SAC Operations," (Extract from Daily Staff Digest, dated 23 May 58), signed by Major General Luehman. [W.V. O'Brien, "Legitimate Military Necessity in Nuclear War," in 2 *World Polity* (1960), 115 n. 20.]

new and different sources of conflict appear. Racial hatred, the jealousy and unforgiving urge for revenge of the underprivileged against their former colonialist and neo-colonialist masters, even the spectre of aggressive nationalism of the kind that produced two world wars confront us in a time when nuclear proliferation is a constantly increasing threat. The distance is enormous between our world of conflict and the international order based on trust and brotherhood to which the teachings of the Church direct us.

(2) Modern nuclear weapons and delivery systems make general nuclear war self-defeating politically and militarily. Yet the possession and deployment of nuclear deterrence systems seems to be the unavoidable alternative to acceptance of domination by the enemies who differ so fundamentally in their views about the nature of man and society. This is the case for both (and there may soon be more than two or three) sides of the balance of terror. For those in the West, possession of a sufficient nuclear deterrent system and the will to make it credible are widely believed to be the price of freedom from totalitarian Communist conquest.

(3) It is necessary to remember that there are few present indications that the political-military situation will produce utilization of nuclear weapons systems except as part of the execution of the deterrent threat. In the light of U.S. behavior since 1945 and of Soviet behavior since 1949 there is little reason to believe that either would initiate a general nuclear war. That is not the most pressing problem. The problem is that of preventing events that were not intended to reach the proportions of a nuclear war from triggering one. The basic moral question arising from the factual situation is: Does morality permit the continuance of the nuclear deterrent balance of terror, requiring as it does the credible willingness to wage the nuclear war that none of the nuclear powers wants to wage and which the deterrent is designed to prevent?

Before confronting this issue, however, we should first review the teaching of the Church on war.

3
Traditional Catholic
Thought: The Just War

Catholic thought on war may be traced through the following periods:

(1) The Early Church to the time of St. Augustine;

(2) The period from St. Augustine to St. Thomas;

(3) The period from St. Thomas through the Renaissance, approximately to the early 17th century;

(4) The period of comparative inactivity with respect to studies of the moral implications of war, roughly the 17th to the 20th century;

(5) The period of gradual revival of just war theories and of interest in international law and organization following World War I to the end of World War II;

(6) Catholic reactions to the threat of nuclear war, 1945 to the present.

Part of the problem of contemporary efforts to deal with modern war can be quickly indicated by evaluating the productivity and creativity of these six periods. The period of the Early Church tends to support pacifist attitudes and provides little assistance to those seeking guidelines for the moral conduct of war. The second and third periods, spanning the Middle Ages and the Renaissance are the periods of greatest contributions to Catholic teaching on war and remain even today the cornerstone of official Catholic doctrine on the subject. The three hundred years of the fourth period represent an unfortunate combination of developments: realistic and imaginative studies of the morality of war declined in quantity and quality just as modern technology and politico-ideological trends moved man toward the theory and practice of total war. The fifth, the inter-war period, produced little more than the restatement of the traditional just war doctrine without substantial recognition of the impact of modern war. Its emphasis, like that of most contemporary thought on war and peace, was on the elimination of war through international law and organization. The last period, that of the reaction to nuclear war, will be treated in the next chapter in the context of our analysis of the five preceding periods.

Origins of the Just War Doctrine

Doctrine, attitudes and individual behavior in the Early Church tended toward pacifism or, at least, aloofness from war. There are several reasons for this.

First, Christ was the Prince of Peace. He said: ". . . Blessed are the meek, for they shall possess the earth. . . . Blessed are the peacemakers, for they shall be called children of God. Blessed are they who suffer persecution for justice's sake, for theirs is the kingdom of Heaven" (Mt. 5, 4-10). Vivid in the minds of all Christians is Jesus' rebuke to his followers who would have defended him in the garden: "Those who live by the sword will perish by the sword."

Of course, even the relevant sources in the New Testament provide arguments for the possibility of a just war. Christ himself drove the money changers from the Temple. He supported the public order with the advice to "render unto Caesar the things that are Caesar's." Critics of the early pacifist attitudes also note the incident of the good centurion and conclude that a military career and morality are not necessarily incompatible. Moreover, the Old Testament records blood-curdling acts of war which seem to have enjoyed divine toleration. There seems to be room for both pacifist and just war interpretations of sacred scripture. There is little explicit guidance on the problems of public or group morality in the bible, particularly in the New Testament. The emphasis is upon individual morality. It remains an historic fact, however, that the early Christians tended to draw a pacifist or isolationist message from the teachings of the Church.

A second set of reasons for the early Christians' aloofness from war is extremely practical. They emphasized the overwhelming importance of man's destiny to share in the kingdom of heaven. They scorned the things of this world, whose early end some of them awaited. They viewed Roman society as pagan, corrupt, sinful and dangerously hostile, and obviously had ample grounds for such judgments. Therefore the early Christians tended to concentrate on personal and sectarian sanctity rather than on the reform of the pagan society which either scorned or persecuted them. Finally, actual military service involved objectionable practices ranging from worship of pagan gods to risking the occasions of sin endemic in the military life of the day.

However, the forces of history worked against the continuation of this unnatural separation of Christians from society and its problems. After his victory at Milvian Bridge (312 A.D.), which he attributed to divine intervention, Emperor Constantine was dramatically converted to a disposition favorable to Christianity. On February 27, 380 A.D. the Emperor Theodosius I was to declare Christianity the official religion of the Empire. The fate of Christianity increasingly appeared to be tied to that of the Empire. The decline of the Empire and the invasions of pagan barbarians confronted the Church with the choice of assisting in the defense of Roman society or of waiting tremulously to see what life would be like under the barbarians. The Church clearly chose the former course.

From St. Augustine to St. Thomas

From the standpoint of formal doctrine, the teaching of the Church on morality and war began with the writings of St. Augustine (354-430 A.D.). He lived at a time when the Roman Empire had already suffered a number of invasions, with more in prospect. In his writings and letters of counsel he emphatically justified Christian participation in wars when the cause was just. Thus began the Christian "just war" tradition (a pagan, classical just war tradition had already developed in Graeco-Roman times). [See St. Augustine, *The City of God,* trans. Marcus Dods, DD. (2 vols. New York: Hafner, 1948), I, 21; XIX, 7; Paul Ramsey, *War and the Christian Conscience* (Durham, North Carolina: Duke University Press, 1961), Ch. II; Richard Shelly Hartigan, "Saint Augustine on War and Killing: The Problems of the Innocent," in 27 *Journal of the History of Ideas* (April-June, 1966), pp. 195-204.]

In eight centuries between St. Augustine's time and that of St. Thomas Aquinas (1224-1274) the principal teachings, attitudes and activities of the Church reaffirmed the concept of just war. St. Augustine's views seem to have prevailed in Scholastic thought. There was a whole network of mutual support between chivalry and other feudal institutions, and both the Church as an institution and Christianity as a religion. The central figure in this complex was the knight in armor. Ultimately the Church was to call upon the resources of this knightly tradition in the crusades. The popes and the hierarchy often made use of war as an instrument of their own policies wherein the religious and temporal elements were frequently mixed.

During the same centuries the Church attempted to restrict the objects of warlike acts, the frequency and duration of wars, and some of the means of war. The Peace of God, *e.g.,* Council of Charroux, 988 A.D., emphasized the sacredness of the lives of Christians and laid down prohibitions against attacks on churches, clerics, and the common people who were considered non-combatants. The Truce of God, *e.g.,* Council of Clermont, 1095 A.D., reiterated the prescriptions of the Peace of God and sought to reduce the number of days when fighting was permitted by a complicated ban on fighting on various days and seasons particularly revered in the Church's calendar. Efforts were made to proscribe weapons that were deemed unworthy of the traditions of chivalry, *e.g.,* the ban on the cross bow by the Lateran Council, 1139 A.D. However ineffectual these measures might seem to modern critics, they represent significant efforts to civilize "Christians" who were very close to the barbarism of their forebears. Any suggestion that the fierce behavior of these warriors was softened by religion has to be considered encouraging. But the significant point is that these efforts to limit war occurred in a doctrinal and operational context wherein just wars were condoned. The problems of morality and war were apparently seen primarily as problems of limitation rather than elimination.

Moreover, it must be admitted that Church teaching at this time was very far from insisting on limitations on war derived from a universal natural law applicable to *all* men. The various limitations on the conduct of war proclaimed by the Church applied only to Christians. Infidels did not benefit from them. It should also be noted that the greatest interest in limiting war was shown with respect to persons and property directly connected with the Church.

That peace, not war, was still the generally preferred goal of the Church becomes clear in St. Thomas: reformulation of the Augustinian just war theory. By the way in which St. Thomas raises the question, we are led to believe that the presumption is *against* the morality of war. He began by asking whether war was ever *not sinful*. To be just, a war had to overcome a presumption of sinfulness. He concluded that sometimes war is not sinful and proceeded to lay down three conditions for a just war:

(1) declaration by a competent authority;

(2) just cause;

(3) right intention. (St. Thomas, *Summa Theologica, Secunda Secundae* Qu. 40.)

These conditions remain the core of the just war's requirements with respect to the decision to go to war. However, St. Thomas does not concern himself explicitly with the morality of the means of war, except for scattered marginal questions, *e.g.,* the sinfulness of ambushes.

The Late Scholastics and the Just War Theory in Modern Times

In the 16th and 17th centuries, Francisco de Vitoria (1483-1586), Francisco Suarez (1548-1617) and other Scholastics developed and refined the Augustinian-Thomistic just war theory. [See Francisco de Vitoria, "De Indis et de Iure Belli Selectiones," being parts of *Selectiones Theologicae XII,* ed. Ernest Nys; trans. John Pawley Bate with a revised text by Herbert Francis Wright in *The Classics of International Law,* ed. James Brown Scott (Washington: Carnegie Endowment for International Peace, 1917). Also see Francisco Suarez, S.J., "Selections From Three Works — De Legibus, Ac Deo Legislatore, Defensio Fidei Catholicae et Apostolicae Adversus Anglicanae Sectae Errores," and "De Triplici Virtute Theologica Fide, Spe, et Caritate," in *The Classics of International Law,* ed. James Brown Scott (2 vols., Oxford: At the Clarendon Press; London: Humphrey Milford, 1944). Fr. Suarez' treatment of the just war is found in Disputation XIII: De Bello from "De Caritate" of the last of the three works.]

The principal contribution of these Scholastics, insofar as our modern problems are concerned, lay in the more explicit development of the rules governing the means of war. The later Scholastics are also more explicit in their recognition of the legitimate requirements of military necessity for the just belligerent if he is to have a chance of achieving his just objectives. We shall return to these themes in the summary of conditions for the just war that follows:

Comparatively little of importance was added to the just war theory after the time of Suarez. Thus there occurred an unfortunate failure to develop the theory creatively so as either to adjust or to stand in firm opposition to the various changes in the nature of war that were introduced from the time of the Napoleonic wars through World War I. Even had the just war doctrine been "up to date" in 1914 we would patently have problems in applying it to nuclear war. As it is, we face modern problems with doctrine which in most respects was "perfected" by the 17th century.

The Conditions for a Just War

The conditions for a just war have been variously distinguished from St. Thomas' three to Father McKenna's seven, to take one modern example. There is merit, however, in approaching the problem in terms of two categories borrowed from the positive law of nations:

(1) the *jus ad bellum,* the law governing recourse to armed coercion;

(2) the *jus in bello,* the law governing the means used in war.

The *jus ad bellum* conditions for a just war are as follows:

(1) *Competent Authority.* War must be fought on the order of competent authority. It must serve *public,* not *private* purposes. The wholesale killing and destruction of war can be justified only by its public purpose and only the highest public authority has the right to decide when war is required in the public interests. It is to be hoped that this condition will not be of major concern with respect to nuclear war and deterrence. It should be noted that this condition is not always easily interpreted in cases of guerilla warfare waged by unrecognized insurgents.

(2) *Just Cause.* The condition of just cause includes the following requirements:

(a) There must be a real and grave wrong to be righted or right to be defended. Existence of such a just cause, in turn, may justify:

(i) war of self-defense against invasion;

(ii) offensive war undertaken to obtain by force cessation of wrongs, restitution for past wrongs, and assurances that injuries will not recur;

(iii) offensive war undertaken not only to assert the just belligerent's rights but to support justice generally (wars of vindictive justice), *e.g.,* wars against infidels and heretics. (It should be noted that this is an historical, *not* a contemporary example.)

(b) *Proportionality.* Careful calculation is required from the authorities initiating a just war to determine its likely evil effects and their proportionality to the just causes. These calculations are obviously extremely difficult.

Some authorities require moral certitude of greater good than evil resulting from a just war. Some are satisfied with the "probability" of greater good. (This is an ancient and extremely difficult subject which we note here without encouraging expectations that authoritative resolution will soon be forthcoming.) This is obviously an important problem in evaluating nuclear war or deterrence, particularly when the evil consequences are so well-known and so great.

Closely related to the foregoing is the requirement that the just party have a reasonable chance of success. History does not unfold an unbroken record of victories by belligerents whose cause appears to have been just. If there is little prospect of success for the just, it would seem probable that this factor would influence the calculations wherein likely good and evil are balanced.

A further dimension in the calculation of the probability of success is found in wars of self-defense against aggression. Most authorities hold that the victim of aggression has a right to defend itself without regard to its chances of success, *i.e.,* even "hopeless" wars of self-defense may be undertaken as a matter of right. On the other hand, there must be some limit to the risks that a victim of aggression should be permitted to incur if they gravely threaten the rights or existence of the other members of the international community and the international common good.

(c) *Exhaustion of Peaceful Remedies.* No matter how solid the grounds for a just war, the just party must have made every reasonable effort to obtain satisfaction by peaceful means. To use the language of modern international law, all peaceful remedies must have been exhausted.

(3) *Right Intention.* A just belligerent must have right intention. Among the components of this condition are the following:

(a) The just party must continue the war only so long as it is necessary to obtain the just goals for which it was initiated. Once a war is pressed beyond that point in pursuit of unjust or insufficiently grave goals it becomes unjust.

(b) Nothing must be done to imperil the ultimate object of every just war, namely, the establishment of a just and lasting peace. Thus if the conduct of the war is needlessly brutal or the peace terms patently unfair, sentiments of hatred and desire for revenge may be encouraged in the defeated nation.

(c) Finally, an initially just war must not be permitted to become the occasion for indulgence in unjust and uncharitable attitudes and practices, of the kind that tend to be unleashed in wartime.

All these elements in the concept of right intention merge into the limitations of the *jus in bello* governing the means of war. Obviously the goals set and the intentions and psychological dispositions of the belligerents have critical effect on the means used and the manner of their use.

The *jus in bello* takes two forms: the principle of proportionality and the prohibitions or limitations of the use of particular means.

As with the requirement that there be a reasonable *proportionality* between the reasons for going to war and the likely results, there must also be proportionality between the means used and the likely results in terms of accomplishing just ends. Like any domestic law concept of reasonableness, whether it be a "reasonable" way of driving an automobile under difficult weather conditions or a reasonable reaction of a houseowner to apprehending an armed robber in his basement, determination of reasonable proportionality is difficult to discuss in general terms. This difficulty, however, does not relieve the conscientious decision-maker from attempting the calculation. We shall return to this subject when we discuss the proportionality of specific forms of nuclear war and deterrence.

With respect to prohibitions or limitations on particular means of war, the means used in a just war must themselves be morally permissible. No intrinsically immoral means may be used, no matter how effective they promise to be nor how just the objectives of the war. This is at the heart of our problem of morality and nuclear war. To the extent that the morality of certain acts of nuclear war and deterrence turn on the principle of proportionality, many potential permissible and forbidden situations can be hypothesized. But if, for one reason or another, nuclear war is found to be intrinsically immoral, *malum in se,* no use of such a means would ever be moral.

The most important characterization of an act as intrinsically immoral concerns the killing of "innocents" (as the just war theorists termed them) or "non-combatants" (as they are commonly called today, particularly in international law). Non-combatants are to be immune from direct, intentional attack. The rationale for this rule is:

(1) Generally speaking, it is never permitted for man to usurp God's dominion over human life by killing another man.

(2) Exceptions to this rule arise because of the exigencies of political society. Disturbers of the peace, whether within a society or when attacking it as outside aggressors, imperil the lives and rights of its peaceful inhabitants. This engenders in the forces of public law and order (as well as in the citizenry in exceptional circumstances) the right and duty of defending that order, if necessary by killing outlaws or enemy aggressors. But there obviously is no right to kill human beings who have not given rise by their actions to this exceptional right of the police or soldiers.

Scholastic tradition has held from St. Thomas' time to the present that, under the principle of double effect,* innocents might be attacked and even killed if the primary intent was the accomplishment of the licit elimination of the aggressor and the injury to the innocent was only incidental. Thus the Scholastics condoned the use of catapults to throw projectiles into a fortress under siege even though it could be expected that at least some innocents would be hit.

This distinction between the direct, intentional and the incidental, unintended killing of innocents was reasonably meaningful because of the state of the art of war at the time. When St. Thomas wrote, the knight on horseback was the key to victory, cavalry was the decisive arm. Aside from the problems of the siege, most combat was man-to-man and respect for the requirements of the Peace of God with respect to the immunity of clerics and the common people was presumably quite feasible. However, the devastating effects of three new methods of warfare gradually reduced the supremacy of the knight on horseback, of cavalry, and of the virtually impregnable castles from which they operated. The development of the English long bow employed by irregular foot soldiers drawn from the common people (*e.g.,* Crecy, 1346 and Agincourt, 1415), the impact of the tactics of the Swiss infantry armed with long pikes, and the use of gun-

---

* St. Thomas himself did not apply the principle of double effect to noncombatant immunity, a subject with which he did not deal.

powder against castles (*e.g.,* in the capture of Constantinople by the Turks in 1453) all changed the nature of war. Among other things, these developments increased the number of belligerents and the territorial scope of their activities. They also hastened the trend toward popular rather than aristocratic armies. By the time Suarez was continuing the just war tradition in the late 16th and early 17th centuries, the likelihood of "incidental, unintended" killing of innocents in normal military operations had greatly increased. The need for the qualifying double effect clause to the non-combatant immunity rule was firmly established. However, whether the double effect concept is sufficient to justify the use of modern means of war whose lethal effects on non-combatants are better described as "inevitable" than "incidental" remains to be seen.

Just War and Natural Law Concepts in International Law, 1625-1945

The just war doctrine was to have a mixed fate. As the modern state system emerged in the 17th century, international law also developed. Prominent in early international law was a secular just war doctrine, *e.g.,* Grotius' *De Jure Belli ac Pacis (1625)*. Most of it was either taken from the Scholastic just war doctrine or resembled it substantially. But the very introduction of the doctrine into positive international law tended to bring it into disrepute.

The Scholastic just war doctrine was developed for the *moral* guidance of statesmen and responsible citizens. Its *sanction* was, in the final analysis, a supernatural one. Although there was in the doctrine provision for enforcement of justice by an individual country, the main focus of the doctrine was on the *conscience* of the statesman, in those days generally a "Prince."

The just war doctrine in international law was a legal, not a moral doctrine. But since there was no final authority to judge the legitimacy of wars and no international authority to enforce such judgment, the effectiveness of the just war system depended on the honesty and justice of the various powers. In fact, they misused the doctrine. Cynical claims of just war had become so numerous by the 19th century that the just war doctrine, together with related natural law concepts, was generally ridiculed.

In the 19th century international law recognized the right of any sovereign state to go to war for any, or no, reason. The law was only concerned with regulating the conduct of war, protecting neutral rights, and terminating wars in an orderly manner. The notion that wars could be just or unjust, legally or morally, was relegated to the category of foolish "medieval" double talk, like disputing how many angels could dance on the head of a pin! There was a general disregard for the whole Scholastic natural law tradition and a great belief in inevitable progress through purely human, "scientific" advances in knowledge and in political, economic and social organization. The principle of non-combatant immunity from direct attack was firmly established in both customary and conventional international law.

But the notion of just war, like many other natural law concepts, was to be revived in our century. As a result of the breakdown of a predominately secular and humanistic worldview and its distinctive international system in World War I, the League of Nations was formed with the basic purpose of preventing recurrence of war. In principle, states no longer had the legal right to go to war except in self-defense or in support of the international order. This was the goal of such important international agreements as the Kellogg-Briand Peace Pact of 1928. After World War II this trend was consolidated in the United Nations system (as well as in regional systems such as the OAS and NATO). The Nuremberg and other war crimes trials reiterated the commitment of the victorious powers to these principles. The only "legal" wars under the UN system are "police" actions fought on order of the UN or other appropriate international body, or wars of individual or collective self-defense against aggression. Unlike the old system of the 19th century, there are legal and illegal wars. Many international law authorities have noted a striking resemblance between these legal concepts and the moral concepts of just and unjust wars.

The unusual barbarity of World War II has produced a further revival of interest in just war theories. The common man sees

wars as the usual outgrowth of international politics; like death
and taxes they are always with us. Thus there continues to be
much skepticism about the feasibility of the UN system limiting
the right to go to war. But ordinary men all over the world saw
in the excesses of World War II something that was terrible
and *unnatural*. It took a war in which things were done to human
beings which by *any* standard are contrary to "higher" or "natural
law" to encourage renewed interest in the just war concepts of war
as a morally limited institution. [See Myres S. McDougal and
Florentino P. Feliciano, *Law and Minimum World Public Order:
The Legal Regulation of International Coercion* (New Haven:
Yale University Press, 1961); Wolfgang Friedmann, *The Changing Structure of International Law* (New York: Columbia University Press, 1964); and Julius Stone, *Legal Controls of International Conflict* (New York: Rinehart, 1959).]

The inability of secular positivism to provide an adequate basis
for normative analysis of questions of war and peace, and the
excesses of modern war have, in effect, given Catholic and other
natural law doctrines of just war another chance to contribute
to the efforts to curb war. But the serious question we must discuss in this book is: Now that we may be asked to discuss the
morality of war, what do we answer?

*Some Difficulties of Applying the Just War
Doctrine to Modern War*

Before we consider the reaction of Catholic thinkers to modern
war, we must note the difficulties of applying the traditional just
war doctrine to modern war.

The actors in war have changed greatly in our times. For the
"Prince" we must substitute a variety of types of governments
ranging from democratic to totalitarian. For the military com-
mander and the individual soldier we must substitute in everything except tactical combat, immense "war efforts" comprising
intricate networks of a military, political and economic nature.

The avowed causes for war have changed considerably. States

still blend a legalistic-moral element in their explanations for war-like behavior but the reasons for recourse to war are much more complex than "righting a wrong" or "obtaining restitution." On the other hand, sweeping claims to war on behalf of "justice" are on the increase.

The means of war have changed so drastically as to raise the question as to how a doctrine conceived in terms of earlier means can be made relevant to our problems. Among the most important changes are the following:

(1) Until well toward the end of the last century the principal means of warfare involved direct, personal combat or the direct aiming of projectiles at objects within eyesight. In these circumstances the problem of distinguishing the non-combatant from the combatant was not substantially different from what it had been in the 13th or 17th centuries. With the appearance of modern artillery, then of aircraft and submarines, war became increasingly impersonal, waged at long range by calculation and with means that frequently destroyed within such a large area that they could not be relied upon to spare non-combatants or non-military targets.

(2) This trend was further advanced by the entrance of a significant part of the "non-combatant" population into the "war effort" with the result that they were no longer treated as non-combatants but as legitimate objects of attack. The traditional prohibition against direct attack on non-combatants was already potentially in conflict with the *inherent* qualities of modern weapons at least by World War I. The mass destruction of cities in World War II saw the abandonment of any pretense at retaining the distinction.

(3) In the nuclear age, there are small, "tactical" nuclear weapons which could be used in some regions in such a way as to distinguish between combatants and non-combatants, military and non-military targets. However, given the characteristics of the large H-bombs, nuclear deterrence based on such weapons requires a willingness to ignore these distinctions. Such weapons are maintained for the purpose of *not* being used, but still they *are* deployed for retaliation to aggression.

We may, therefore, summarize our moral dilemma as follows:

(1) In the days in which the just war doctrine was developed

it was quite possible to observe the restrictions of the doctrine
and still have a reasonable chance of winning.

(2) Today, a party which adhered strictly to the traditional
doctrine, particularly on the point of non-combatant immunity
from direct attack, would stand no chance either of deterring or
fighting a nuclear war with a nuclear enemy.

(3) In *all* present forms of warfare — so-called conventional,
sub-conventional guerilla or irregular — literal application of the
rule against intentional, direct attack on non-combatants (even
if one could form a satisfactory definition for true non-combatants
in modern wars) would make moral engagement in warfare virtually impossible. Finally, it is questionable whether some of the
forms of social protest that have been applauded by enlightened
Christians can avoid direct, intentional attacks on innocents.

In the first place, it is not uncommon for political-social protests
to take the form of riots in which those identified in some way
with the opponents of revolutionary change are attacked together
with innocent third parties who are on the scene. In such cases
the leaders of the protest actions are in a very real sense violating
the concept underlying the immunity of innocents from intentional
direct attack. If the principle is valid in wars between nations,
why should it be less valid in civil wars or domestic political-
social protests? In the second place, even non-violent protests
often lead to death or injury to innocents. In these cases, to be
sure, the persons who actually do the injury are the resisting hostile
crowd or the police. But the organizer of the non-violent demon-
stration knows the dangers of the situation when he begins it.
The leader who sends little children or defenseless men and woman
down a street toward snarling police dogs, mounted troopers and
howling mobs surely knows that the probable result of his decision
will be serious injury and possible death to the innocent.

Let us look, now, at the Catholic reaction to this and other
dilemmas of the age of conflict and nuclear war.

4

Catholic Teaching and Nuclear War

The Catholic reaction, official, semi-official, and lay, to the moral dilemmas posed by nuclear war has been uneven, inconclusive and unsatisfactory. A number of different factors contributed to this state of affairs. It is difficult to judge the importance of each factor but they include the following:

(1) Throughout the nuclear age Catholics have been particularly concerned with the threat of Communist imperialism and subversion. The defense of the Christian world since 1945 has, in large measure, rested first upon fission and then upon thermonuclear power. Catholics have agreed with at least one element in the slogan, "Better Red Than Dead," *viz.,* the assumption that if one does not risk nuclear "death" one *will* be "red," under Communist tyranny. (The anti-Communist factor is, however, changing in content and importance as the Communist world divides and changes and as Catholic attitudes, particularly since Pope John's pontificate, become more flexible. But it is fair to say that anti-Communist attitudes strongly dominated Catholic thinking on war and deterrence until quite recently.)

(2) Like many statesmen, intellectuals and experts in international relations, Catholics have tended to get around the question of the morality of nuclear war by emphasizing the necessity for avoiding war through international law and organization, and worldwide political, economic and social reforms. While such goals involve the ultimate answers to our problems of war and peace, concentration on them to the neglect of the morality of war and deterrence results in a vacuum wherein the Christian is left without adequate guidance.

A study of the literature on the subject confirms the suspicion that the complexities and horrors of the subject matter have discouraged systematic research and thought on morality, nuclear war and deterrence, either by individuals or organizations. The literature abounds with occasional flashes of light from a writer who then disappears, insofar as this subject is concerned, for years at a time. Meanwhile the problems continue.

This lack of systematic study is reflected in the comparative sparsity of official church pronouncements on the subject and of the often unsatisfactory nature of official pronouncements when they are forthcoming. This is not surprising. Statements by popes and bishops do not appear abruptly. They usually represent long years of study and reflection by experts until a high Church official deems it proper to apply the findings, in the light of his own insights, to a pressing problem.

To write about the morality of modern war one must know a good deal about modern war itself. It is not enough to master the basic facts and issues as they stand at a particular moment. Those who discuss morality and war must be constantly learning more, keeping up with developments in the fields of weapons systems, strategy, the overall trends of international politics, and the evolving trends in efforts on behalf of international law and organization.

Thus an analysis written at a time when the full implications of the missile age were still not clear might conclude by condemning some forms of nuclear war as immoral but also hold that certain forms of limited nuclear war could conceivably be moral. This might be useful guidance for the period in which it was written but it would not help us to answer the moral questions raised by our present-day deterrent forces and the balance of nuclear terror. The person who wants to keep up with the problem must always ask himself, "Does this moral analysis deal with the real problems as they presently confront us?" If the answer is negative the analysis may give insights into parts of our problem but it cannot give a comprehensive answer. It is hard to say if this open-ended process, in which morality re-examines runaway technology and rapid and profound political developments, will ever become sufficiently stabilized to allow a gifted theologian to write the "definitive" book on the subject. It would be prudent not to wait for such a book before tackling the problem!

Since Hiroshima the popes have lamented the threat of nuclear war in increasingly strong terms. Pleas to end the threat of nuclear and of all wars have generally been made in the context of appeals to eliminate the causes of war through disarmament, the development of international law and organization and the establishment of social justice throughout the world. None of the recent popes has attempted a full-scale re-examination of the just war doctrine in the light of nuclear problems. Even the work of Vatican Council II on this subject represents only a beginning.

The Popes on Nuclear War and Deterrence

The most definite statement of Pope Pius XII was made in 1954 in an address to the Delegates to the Eighth Congress of the World Medical Association in Rome. He condemned all modern "total" wars except in self-defense, when war is "forced upon one by an obvious, extremely serious and otherwise unavoidable injustice." Thus an offensive war that would have been "just" in earlier times is no longer permitted. ABC weapons (atomic-bacteriological-chemical) might be used, said the Pope, in wars of self-defense. "Even then, however, one must strive to avoid it by all possible means through international understandings or to impose limits on its use that are so clear and rigorous that its effects remain restricted to the strict demands of defense. When, moreover, putting this method to use involves such an extension of the evil that it entirely escapes from the control of man, its use must be rejected as immoral . . ." Such means, concluded Pius XII, are "not permitted for any reason whatsoever." [Pius XII, Address to Delegates to the Eighth Congress of the World Medical Association, in Rome, September 30, 1954, trans. National Catholic Welfare Conference News in *Pattern for Peace,* ed. Harry F. Flannery (Westminster, Md.: Newman Press, 1962), pp. 236-40.]

This is a strong statement, but it still leaves our questions in doubt. *When* does a weapon (or weapons system) "entirely escape control"? Have ours already escaped control? Some have said that the strategic weapons systems escape control by their very nature. Authoritative interpreters of Pius XII's thought, such as Father Gustav Gundlach, say that the weapons are under control if those who possess and deploy them have a rational, proportionate purpose. [See Gustav Gundlach, S.J., "Pie XII et la Guerre Atomique," in *Documents au Sommaire, Revue des questions allemandes* (May-June, 1959), pp. 268-84; Robert Bosc, S.J., *La Société internationale et l'Eglise,* (Paris: Institut Catholique de Paris, Institut d'Etudes Sociales, Action Populaire, Bibliotheque de la Recherche Sociale, 1960), pp. 84-8, and references to Fr. Gundlach's writings in Germany cited therein.]

While no pope has explicitly endorsed any particular form of nuclear warfare (except in the broad, and, as Father John Courtney Murray has said, "tortured" terms of Pius XII's admission of the possibility of legitimate use of atomic weapons in defense),* strong endorsement of "limited nuclear war" was forthcoming in the late fifties and early sixties from eminent theologians such as Father Murray and some German theologians. The influential Catholic layman, Thomas E. Murray of the Atomic Energy Commission, was a leader of efforts to devise limited means of nuclear defense. It is not difficult to imagine limited means of nuclear war that would satisfy the moral-legal standards of "reasonableness" in a given situation. But limited nuclear war as a concept is vulnerable on several grounds, the most important being that of the danger of escalation. This means that if atomic or nuclear weapons were once introduced there would be no reason to expect that the parties would not keep "upping the ante" until they were fighting a general nuclear war, something that many who favor limited nuclear war would condemn as immoral. In any event, today one cannot hold a theory of limited nuclear war without first taking a compatible position on strategic nuclear deterrence. Hence any treatment which deals only with limited nuclear war in a vacuum is not adequate.

Pope John XXIII dealt with the problem of nuclear deterrence as such. In *Pacem in Terris* the late Pope said that it is difficult to imagine anyone starting a nuclear war, that in the nuclear age

* Address to the Catholic Association for International Peace, October 24, 1958 and reproduced in numerous symposia.

war is no longer a reasonable instrument of policy. Pope John called upon all "men of good will" to move the world from the balance of terror to a peace based on trust. He even seemed to deprecate extreme versions of the nature of the Communist threat. But the Pope did not clearly condemn nuclear war as immoral. (His characterization of it as unreasonable is not substantially different from statements along the same lines by Khrushchev, Eisenhower, Kennedy, and others.) His overall advice was to move step by step toward arms control and disarmament and not to expect that all problems could be solved by revolutionary, sweeping changes. Thus *Pacem in Terris* upsets the moral, doctrinaire and zealous anti-Communists but it is far from giving comfort to Catholic pacifists and advocates of unilateral disarmament. Even after the strong pleas of the encyclical for a serious effort at arms control, Catholics remain free to hold a broad variety of opinions about the morality of nuclear war, deterrence, preparations and the possession of nuclear weapons.

In the light of the foregoing considerations, we turn now to a summary analysis of the teachings of the three popes of the nuclear age, as they relate to the conditions and rules of the just war theory. Setting aside the condition of competent authority which does not seem to be relevant to nuclear war as distinguished from some of the sub-conventional forms of conflict presently flourishing, let us consider just cause.

The first point to make is that the popes agree that just defensive wars are still possible and necessary. Injustices are being perpetrated that are sufficiently grave to warrant recourse to war by the victims. The prospects are clearly for an indefinite continuation of this state of affairs. Even though the dangers of modern war require a drastic tightening in interpretations of the condition of grave injustice, the popes all have been able to envisage the necessity for just wars of some kind.

In his 1948 Christmas Message Pope Pius XII stated:

> One thing, however, is certain: the commandment of peace is a matter of divine law. Its purpose is the protection of the goods of humanity, inasmuch as they are gifts of the Creator. Among these goods some are of such importance for society, that it is perfectly lawful to defend them against

unjust aggression. Their defense is even an obligation for the nations as a whole who have a duty not to abandon a nation that is attacked.

The certainty that this duty will not go unfulfilled will serve to discourage the aggressor and thus war will be avoided or, if the worst should come, its sufferings will at least be lessened.*

In an address emphasizing the criminality of aggressive war, *i.e.,* "of making a modern war which is not required by absolute necessity of self-defense and which brings with it, as We can assert without hesitation, unthinkable ruin, suffering and horrors," the Pope went on to say:

> The community of nations must reckon with unprincipled criminals who, in order to realize their ambitious plans, are not afraid to unleash total war. This is the reason why other countries, if they wish to preserve their very existence and their most precious possessions, and unless they are prepared to accord free action to international criminals, have no alternative but to get ready for the day when they must defend themselves. This right to be prepared for self-defense cannot be denied, even in these days, to any state. That, however, does not in any way alter the fact that unjust war is to be accounted as one of the very gravest crimes which international penal law must proscribe, must punish with the heaviest penalties, and the authors of which are in every case guilty and liable to the punishment that has been agreed upon. (*Ibid.,* p. 199.)

In his address, "The Threat of ABC Warfare," Pius XII observed that his efforts on behalf of an effective proscription of such weapons nevertheless "always [recognized] the principle of legitimate self-defense."

The strongest reaffirmation by Pius XII of the just defensive war concept was made after the Hungarian Revolt was crushed by Soviet intervention in 1956. In his Christmas Message of that year the late Holy Father said:

* Pius XII, Christmas Message Broadcast to the Whole World, December 23, 1948, in *Pattern for Peace: Catholic Statements on International Order,* ed. Harry W. Flannery (Westminster, Md.: Newman Press, 1962), p. 171.

We are convinced that today, too, in face of an enemy determined to impose on all peoples, in one way or another, a special and intolerable way of life, only the unanimous and courageous behavior of all who love the truth and the good can preserve peace and will preserve it. It would be a fatal error to repeat what, in similar circumstances, happened during the years preceding the Second World War; when all the threatened nations, and not merely the smallest, sought their safety at the expense of others, using them as shields, so to speak, and even seeking very questionable economic and political advantages from their neighbor's suffering. In the end all together were overwhelmed in the holocaust. . . .

Present day conditions, which find no counterparts in the past, should be clear to everyone. There is no longer room for doubt concerning the aims and methods which rely on tanks, when these latter noisily crash over borders, sowing death in order to force civilian peoples into a pattern of life they explicitly detest; when destroying, as it were, the stages of possible negotiation and mediation, the threat is made of using atomic weapons to gain certain demands, be they justified or not. It is clear that in the present circumstances there can be verified in a Nation a situation, wherein, when every effort to avoid war has been expended in vain, war — for effective self-defense and with the hope of a favorable outcome against unjust attack — could not be considered unlawful. (Pius XII, Christmas Message Broadcast to the Whole World, December 23, 1956, in Flannery, pp. 282, 283.)

This passage was followed by a rejection of conscientious objection to service in just defensive wars forced upon truly representative governments (a position reversed by the Vatican Council). Again, in his Christmas Message of 1957, Pius XII, while pleading for progress toward peace and disarmament pointedly added, "and always allowing for the right of self-defense." (Pius XII, Christmas Message Broadcast to the Whole World, December 22, 1957, in Flannery, p. 295.)

Pope John XXIII in *Pacem in Terris* reaffirmed the right of each state "to existence, to self-development, to the means necessary to its attainment, and to be the one primarily responsible for this self-development." (*Pacem in Terris, Encyclical Letter of Pope John XXIII Art. 86*) The Pope went on to plead for serious efforts at disarmament and the development of international peacekeeping institutions. However he firmly recognized that the starting point for nations in our dangerous world was deterrence and preparations for self-defense. The Pope urged the world to alter this state of affairs but he seems to have recognized that in such a period the right of self-defense remained valid and necessary.

Finally, we should note the realism of Pope Paul VI's address to the United Nations of October 4, 1965. The whole thrust of this address was summed up in the words, "No more war, war never again." But in this eloquent call for peace and for continued faith in the ultimate prospects for success for the peacemakers, the Pope acknowledged that "you are still at the beginnings. Will the world ever succeed in changing that selfish and bellicose mentality which, up to now, has been interwoven in so much of its history? It is hard to foresee; but it is easy to affirm that it is toward that new history, a peaceful, truly human history, as promised by God to men of good will, that we must resolutely march. The roads thereto are already well marked out for you; and the first is that of disarmament."

Thus, shortly after Pope Paul's plea that, "If you wish to be brothers, let the arms fall from your hands," he said: "As long as man remains that weak, changeable and even wicked being that he often shows himself to be, defensive arms will, unfortunately, be necessary." This reaffirms the right of legitimate self-defense in the present world. That right will be altered or removed only as success is achieved in securing what the Pope called, "the ways of guaranteeing the security of international life, without having recourse to arms."

Having established the continued survival of the right of just wars of legitimate self-defense it should not be necessary to belabor the point that this right is considered *exceptional* by modern popes, an unfortunate and lamentable necessity to be condoned in extreme cases. Thus it is quite clear that *offensive* just wars are no longer permitted. As Father Murray said in 1958 in his famous address to the Catholic Association for International Peace:

Modern theory distinguished three reasons for recourse to war by the sovereign state: *ad vindicandas offensiones, ad repetendas res, ad repellendas injurias,* [to punish offenses, to recover losses, to ward off injuries]. Pius XII, it seems to me, outlawed the first two categories of "war aims." The third category is proper to the concept of "defensive" war. At that, the main thrust of his thought on war, viewed in the total context of his dominant concern with international organization, goes against the modern notion of *jus belli* as an inherent attribute of national sovereignty. (Address to the Catholic Association for International Peace, October 24, 1958 and reproduced in numerous symposia.)

If this interpretation, which is supported by *Pacem in Terris,* is correct, the moral right to engage in a just war is the same as the legal right of an individual state to have recourse to armed coercion. In both cases the justification must be self-defense. The only other legally permissible recourse to armed coercion is participation in enforcement actions against aggressors or states producing threats to the peace as determined by the Security Council. Other internationally authorized armed interventions, such as the UN defense of South Korea, really rest on the right of *collective* self-defense in the sense of Article 51 of the UN Charter, not on the right and duty to enforce the decisions of the Security Council. Recent attempts to transfer the legal authority to order what amounts to enforcement in the form of armed intervention to regional organizations such as the Organization of American States in the Dominican Republic are of dubious legal validity.

To concretize the teachings of modern popes on the requirement of just cause, let us consider the problems raised by Castro's Cuba. If Cuba mounted an overt military attack against another Latin American state, or a large-scale indirect aggression joined to an internal insurgency instigated, supported and directed by Cuba, the target state would have a right to fight a just war of self-defense against Cuba — providing the other conditions that we will be reviewing next are met. Under Article 51 of the Charter and under the mutual security provisions of the various OAS pacts, the United States could join in this just defensive war on the side of the victim of aggression. However, neither grave injustices imposed on the Cuban people by the Castro *régime* nor injustices to other people and governments, including Americans and the United States, would engender a right of the United States to go to war with Cuba if these injustices did not take the form of an armed attack, either direct or indirect. Thus had U.S. forces been committed to the support of the Cuban anti-Castro rebels in the Bay of Pigs invasion they would presumably have been engaged in an unjust offensive war which the Church could not approve, no matter how much it might wish to see the Cuban people and their neighbors freed from the unjust activities of the Castro *régime*.

Obviously, no matter how much sense this position makes in terms of avoidance of war that may lead to disproportionate, catastrophic results, it leaves dissatisfied the sincere proponent of maximum justice for all men. This raises a profound doctrinal question: whether the just war doctrine should continue its modern emphasis on "aggression" in the international legal sense as the cause for just defense, or "injustice" in what Father Murray calls the "older, broader Augustinian concept of *causa justa*." Both Pope John XXIII and Pope Paul VI have continued and strengthened the emphasis on aggression as the sole just cause for recourse to armed force, and that widespread injustice is to be tolerated in order to avoid the greater evils of modern war.

Proportionality and Likelihood of Success

If some just wars of self-defense are still possible, indeed necessary, in our world of conflict, the form they might take remains extremely vague in modern thought. We have statements by Pius XII on these subjects. On the proportionality of good and evil results of war he observes:

> Our desire that any war be punished at the international level is not absolutely necessary for the self-defense of a community seriously threatened by an injustice that cannot be prevented in any other way. Even such a war, however, must be waged at the risk of giving a free hand in international affairs to brute violence and lack of conscience. It is not enough, therefore, to have to defend oneself against

just any injustice in order to justify resorting to the violent means of war. When the damages caused by war are not comparable to those of "tolerated injustice," one may have a duty to "suffer the injustice." (Pius XII, Address to Delegates to the Eighth Congress of the World Medical Association, in Rome, September 30, 1954 in Flannery p. 237.)

On the calculus of estimates of success for the just, he states:

Resting for support on God and on the order he established, the Christian will for peace is thus as strong as steel. Its temper is quite different from mere humanitarian sentiment, too often little more than a matter of pure impression, which detests war only because of its horrors and atrocities, its destruction and its aftermath, but not for the added reason of its injustice. Such a sentiment, under a hedonistic and utilitarian disguise, and materialistic in its source, lacks the solid foundation of a strict and unqualified obligation. It creates conditions which encourage the deception resulting from sterile compromise, the attempt to save oneself at the expense of others, and *the success in every case of the aggressor.*

This is so true that neither the sole consideration of the sorrows and evils resulting from war, nor the careful weighing of the act against the advantage, avail to determine finally, whether it is morally licit, or even in certain concrete circumstances obligatory (provided always there be solid probability of success) to repel an aggressor by force of arms. (Pius XII, Christmas Message Broadcast to the Whole World, December 23, 1948 in Flannery, pp. 170-71.)

The overwhelming number of papal statements on war and peace refer to the extreme forms of armed coercion, namely, either "total war" in the World War II sense that we now call "conventional", or general nuclear war, or the even more feared ABC or CBR war. Theories of limited war, either conventional or nuclear, which have occupied national decision-makers, scholars and moralists have received no comment from the popes. We have no suggestion as to the form that "legitimate self-defense" might take and no definition of Pope Paul VI's term "defensive arms." To borrow from the jargon of the national security and arms control experts, the popes have provided no "scenarios" for just wars of legitimate self-defense, fought with defensive weapons. Undoubtedly the best explanation of this state of affairs is Father Murray's. Speaking of the generality of Pius XII's statements he observed:

> . . . the reason for it may lie in the fact that the Pope was forcing himself to face the desperate case. And in desperate cases, in which conscience is perplexed, the wise moralist is chary of the explicit and the nice, especially when the issue, as here, is one of social and not individual morality. In such cases hardly more than a *Grenzmoral* is to be looked for or counseled. In fact, the whole Catholic doctrine of war is hardly more than a *Grenzmoral,* an effort to establish on a minimal basis of reason a form of human action, the making of war, that remains always fundamentally irrational. (Address to the Catholic Association for International Peace, October 24, 1958 and reproduced in numerous symposia.)

In these circumstances it seems best to defer the major part of the discussion of proportionality and likelihood of success to the consideration under the *jus in bello* of the principal means of modern war, and particularly to the possibility that some of them may be *mala in se,* morally unusable and therefore irrelevant to a moral decision to engage in a just war.

Exhaustion of Peaceful Remedies

It is hardly necessary to quote all major papal statements reiterating the moral obligation of states to solve their differences peaceably. The clear obligations of Christian statesmen and citizens are:

(1) Never to have recourse to armed force except in individual self-defense or as part of a validly authorized international peace-keeping operation.

(2) To utilize every available means of settlement of international disputes including negotiation, cooperation with third party mediation, arbitration, submission to international adjudication before the International Court of Justice or other international tribunal, submission to the United Nations in the manner which appears most likely to produce positive results, whether to the

Security Council, the General Assembly, or to the Secretary General, and where appropriate, submission to regional organizations.

These obligations were all asserted by Pope Pius XII. They were reiterated and strengthened by Pope John XXIII in *Pacem in Terris* when he went out of his way to support the UN and to express the wish that it "may become ever more equal to the magnitude and nobility of its tasks," and that "the day [might] soon come when every human being will find therein an effective safeguard for the rights which derive directly from his dignity as a person." (Art. 145.) Finally, the moral imperatives requiring full and honest use of the means available for peaceful settlement of disputes was dramatically emphasized by Pope Paul in his October 4, 1965 visit to the United Nations.

5
Morality and
Nuclear Weapons Systems

Having established that a comparatively limited right of self-defense remains sanctioned by recent popes, we now face the question of what means are morally permissible in such wars. It is important to see to what extent the principle of non-combatant immunity from intentional direct attack is applied. Are the papal pronouncements on nuclear war explicitly based upon the non-combatant immunity concept? Finally we can expect to find analyses of the problem that turn on a judgment that a particular form of warfare could be proportionate to any just end.

Pius XII appears to have held that certain forms of so-called "total wars" of the pre-Hiroshima variety are immoral.

> . . . Fourthly: Within the limits of a new order, founded on moral principles, once the more dangerous principles of armed conflict have been eliminated, there is no place for a total warfare or for a mad rush to armaments. The calamity of a world war, with the economic and social ruin and the moral dissolution and breakdown which follow in its train, cannot be permitted to envelop the human race for a third time. (Pius XII, Christmas Radio Message *Nell' Alba* to the Whole World, December 24, 1941, trans. National Catholic Welfare Conference in Flannery p. 107.)

> If ever a generation has had to appreciate in the depths of its conscience the call: "war on war," it is certainly the present generation. Having passed, as it has, through an ocean of blood and tears in a form perhaps never experienced in past ages, it has lived through the indescribable atrocities with an intensity such that the recollection of so many horrors

45

must remain stamped in its memory, and even in the deepest recesses of its soul, like a picture of a hell against which anyone who cherishes a sense of humanity desires more than anything else to close the door forever. (Pius XII, Christmas Radio Message, December 24, 1944, trans. National Catholic Welfare Conference, in Flannery, p. 126.)

Pius XII also condemned as immoral weapons that escape "entirely from the control of man." He asserted:

One cannot even in principle pose the question of the lawfulness of atomic, bacteriological and chemical warfare except in the case where it must be judged as indispensable in order to defend oneself under the circumstances pointed out above. Even then, however, one must strive to avoid it by all possible means through international understandings or to impose limits on its use that are so clear and rigorous that its effects remain restricted to the strict demands of defense. When, moreover, putting this method to use involves such an extension of the evil that it entirely escapes from the control of man, its use must be rejected as immoral. Here there would no longer be a question of "defense" against injustice or a necessary "safeguarding" of legitimate possessions, but the pure and simple annihilation of all human life within the radius of action. This is not permitted for any reason whatsoever. (Pius XII, Address to Delegates of the Eighth Congress of the World Medical Association, in Rome, September 30, 1954, in Flannery, pp. 236-7.)

This enigmatic statement has left commentators in disagreement as to what is prohibited, and why this form of warfare is prohibited. (See Fathers Gundlach and Bosc in works cited on p. 36.)

Authoritative commentators, including some close to Pius XII, have said that means do not entirely escape from the control of man if those who employ them use them rationally. Others have thought that the Pope meant that there were weapons systems possessed of such horrendous powers that once unleashed they were out of man's control. As we shall see, this issue is raised again at Vatican Council II.

The more important question is probably the second: *Why* is it that the means to which the Pope refers are "not permitted on any account?" Is it because they cannot be used without necessarily killing all non-combatants (however defined) within the great area wherein their effects are distributed with lethal effect? Or is the objection primarily one of intrinsic disproportionality? We do not know whether the main thrust of the objection is in the direction that *some* (possibly only a small minority) non-combatants will inevitably be killed (violation of non-combatant immunity from intentional direct attack), or if it is abhorrence of the widespread death, destruction and contamination that will result, even though the intent is to destroy legitimate military targets and the targets are in fact mainly military (disproportion between means and good end).

The major treatment of this subject by Pope John XXIII in *Pacem in Terris* is no more clear in terms of the traditional just war doctrine. It is, however, more helpful than the teaching of Pius XII in that it explicitly recognizes the issue of nuclear deterrence, as distinguished from use of nuclear weapons in war. Pope John stated:

> Consequently, people live in constant fear lest the storm that every moment threatens should break upon them with dreadful violence. And with good reason, for the arms of war are ready at hand. Even though it is difficult to believe that anyone would deliberately take the responsibility for the appalling destruction and sorrow that war would bring in its train, it cannot be denied that the conflagration may be set off by some unexpected and obscure event. And one must bear in mind that, even though the monstrous power of modern weapons acts as a deterrent, it is to be feared that the mere continuance of nuclear tests, undertaken with war in mind, will prove a serious hazard for life on earth. (*Pacem in Terris,* Art. 111.)

Thus, Pope John found among the "signs of the times" the following convictions:

> Men are becoming more and more convinced that disputes which arise between states should not be resolved by recourse to arms but rather by negotiation.
> It is true that on historical grounds this conviction is based chiefly on the terrible destructive force of modern

arms: and it is nourished by the horror aroused in the mind by the very thought of the cruel destruction and the immense suffering which the use of those armaments would bring to the human family. For this reason it is hardly possible to imagine that in the atomic era war could be used as an instrument of justice.

Nevertheless, unfortunately, the law of fear still reigns among peoples, and it forces them to spend fabulous sums for armaments: not for aggression they affirm — and there is no reason for not believing them — but to dissuade others from aggression.

There is reason to hope, however, that by meeting and negotiating, men may come to discover better the bonds that unite them together, deriving from the human nature which they have in common; and that they may also come to discover that one of the most profound requirements of their common nature is this: that between them and their respective peoples it is not fear which should reign but love, a love which tends to express itself in a collaboration that is loyal, manifold in form and productive of many benefits. (*Ibid.*, Art. 126-129.)

It is difficult to find in these passages a *rationale* for the condemnation of nuclear war based on non-combatant immunity from intentional, direct attack. It would seem rather that the rejection of nuclear war as a suitable means is based on the principle of proportion, both of resort to war to the expected results of war, and of means to just ends. Pope John comes close to saying that nuclear war would be unthinkable. In this he was not alone. President Eisenhower, Premier Khrushchev and hundreds of other world leaders have said that. But he never reaches the point of stating that nuclear war or nuclear deterrence are immoral. His whole emphasis is on encouraging action to reduce and ultimately eliminate the dangers of nuclear war and deterrence rather than to condemn it.

The statements of Pope Paul VI on war and peace are significant in the attention they give to subconventional warfare characterized by guerrilla war and terrorism. Fear that major overt conventional war might lead to nuclear war, as well as the nature of the forces of conflict at work in the underdeveloped world, have made subconventional war the principal form of international conflict. This fact is reflected in the following statement in Pope Paul's Encyclical *Mense Maio* which embraces nuclear war but which singles out guerrilla warfare:

> Today, as if no lesson had been learned from the tragic experiences of the two conflicts which shed blood in the first half of our century, we have the dreadful spectacle in certain parts of the world of antagonism on the increase between peoples, and see repeated the dangerous phenomenon of recourse to arms instead of negotiation to settle the disputes of the opposing parties. This means that populations of entire nations are subjected to unspeakable sufferings, caused by agitation, guerrilla warfare, acts of war, ever growing in extent and intensity, which could at any moment produce the spark for a terrible fresh conflict. (*The Catholic Messenger,* Davenport, Iowa, May 6, 1965, p. 3.)

Guerrilla operations had likewise been denounced in the Pope's Easter Message of April 18, 1965.

Two months later, however, Pope Paul made the strongest and most explicit moral condemnation of nuclear war that has yet been made by a pope. On the occasion of the twentieth anniversary of the dropping of the A-bomb at Hiroshima, the Pope said:

> During these days, as you know, the entire world press has taken note of the twentieth anniversary of the explosion of the atomic bomb at Hiroshima.
>
> We have noted that official ceremonies in the most unhappy city, which has been modernly rebuilt, have been voluntarily and nobly without any political or polemic character whatsoever. And we have observed, looking at some publications which were sent to us, the picture of a group of persons who are crying and praying, honoring the memory of the innumerable victims of the infernal slaughter and imploring humanity and asking God that this butchery of human lives, this outrage against civilization may never repeat itself. This is a pious, human, and moving gesture.
>
> And we, who many times have likewise in various ways desired that atomic weapons may be banned, unite ourselves with the plea and prayer and with that hope with this our humble Sunday prayer.
>
> Let us pray that the world may never again see a disgraceful day such as that of Hiroshima, that men may never again

place their trust, their calculations and their prestige in such nefarious and dishonorable weapons. [Paul VI, Remarks before recitation of the Angelus, August 8, 1965 in 10 *The Pope Speaks* (Summer-Autumn, 1965) pp. 358, 406.]

Certainly this condemnation is grave and unequivocal. Its importance is of the first magnitude for those facing the moral dilemmas of contemporary nuclear war and deterrence. But even this most explicit condemnation of an historical recourse to nuclear weapons is incomplete and unsatisfactory. At least two questions come to mind. First, if it is so clear that the dropping of the "dishonorable" Hiroshima bomb was an "outrage against civilization" how do we explain the failure of previous popes to come to the same conclusion and make their opinion known? Second, why was the bombing of Hiroshima an "outrage"? Because it violated the principle of intentional, direct attack against non-combatants — which it certainly did? Because the destruction of a large city is *in se* wrong? If so, does it make a difference whether it is done by a single kiloton bomb, by thousands of conventional bombs, or as the result of a protracted siege by armies on the ground? Or perhaps, the Pope's judgment is based on the more complex argument of the disproportionality of using this means in the political-military context of Japan's proximity to defeat.

Most recently, Pope Paul, in his address in New York to the United Nations, called for the "brothers" of the world to "let the [offensive] arms fall" from their hands, "especially those terrible arms which modern science has given you . . ." This plea may serve as a transition between an analysis of the papal teaching on morality of nuclear war and deterrence and the closely related but still separate question of the moral imperatives to make progress in disarmament and the strengthening of international law and organization. Let us summarize the main points in this papal teaching on the former subject.

(1) The right of legitimate self-defense is somewhat reluctantly upheld pending the development of adequate collective security, international peacekeeping capabilities, and machinery for peaceful settlement of disputes.

(2) The right to wage offensive just wars is denied.

(3) Aggressive war is held to be as immoral as it is now illegal. Aggressive war, however, is not defined.

(4) Total war, of the kind witnessed in World War II, is condemned. However it is not clear what rights a just defense has if an aggressor unleashes a total war.

(5) Some, but not all, forms of nuclear war are condemned. They are:

(a) Nuclear war with ABC means that "entirely escape from the control of man" (Pius XII).

(b) Destruction of cities as in the case of Hiroshima (Paul VI).

(6) On the other hand, the treatment of the continuing right of self-defense by all of the popes — but most clearly in the case of Pius XII — is sufficiently linked to references to nuclear weapons to imply that some use of nuclear weapons in defense may be licit.

(7) The moral permissibility of reliance on nuclear deterrence has not been treated satisfactorily. Pope Pius XII never came to grips with the problem, probably because the concept of deterrence in the sense of mutual nuclear deterrence by nuclear equals (as distinguished from massive retaliation deterrence against non-nuclear aggression by presumed nuclear inferiors) did not clearly emerge as a problem until the last years of his reign. Pope John XXIII has given the best, most explicit recognition of the problem in *Pacem in Terris*. He made no explicit moral condemnation of any form of nuclear deterrence or of nuclear deterrence in general. What the Pope did insist upon was the grave moral obligation of all men who had it in their power to help move the world from the balance of terror to a safer and better world system. Pope Paul's condemnation of the Hiroshima A-bombing would seem to imply that similar acts involved in carrying out a deterrent threat to respond in kind to an aggressor's attack on cities would be morally wrong. This is not entirely clear, however, since the factual situation in 1945 was not one of nuclear retaliation in kind. Pope Paul's references to undefined "offensive" and "defensive" weapons do not meet the requirements of an inquiry into the moral

limits of defensive deterrence; they do not explicitly address the phenomenon of contemporary nuclear deterrence.

(8) Except for some of Pius XII's statements during World War II with respect to non-combatant immunity from air attacks, reprisals by belligerent occupants, and other direct, intentional attacks, the issue of non-combatant immunity *as such* has not been clarified by papal statements. We cannot say whether the main concern is over the killing of any (even of one) non-combatants, directly and intentionally, or whether it is over the magnitude of non-combatant deaths and sufferings, *e.g.,* in a large city which is also an important military target. Or indeed, whether the nuclear means that are condemned are immoral primarily because of the universal dangers of radioactive fallout. In conclusion we can only say that modern papal thought clearly condemns forms of general nuclear war that are disproportionate to *any* valid end. It is not clear what the status of the principle of non-combatant immunity from direct, intentional attack is at present. Nor is it clear what, if any, exceptions are permitted to the principle in cases of retaliation in kind in pursuit of the right of self-defense.

The Opinion of Scholars and Publicists

Before turning to the treatment of nuclear war and deterrence by Vatican Council II, discussions by scholars and publicists should be noted. The corpus of scholarly and serious literature on the subject appears modest when compared to the literature on other critical social questions such as population control, and economic, social and racial justice. Accordingly, the "schools of thought" distinguished here may reflect only a small and quite random sample of opinion. However, the positions may generally be distinguished as follows:

Total Pacifists. There are those who do not admit the morality of an intentional killing, even for public purposes or self-defense.

Nuclear Pacifists. Nuclear pacifists condemn nuclear war because its indiscriminate character, even when "small" devices are used, appears to preclude adherence to the principle of non-combatant immunity from intentional, direct attack. Persons who hold this position generally assume escalation from limited to unlimited nuclear war under the stress of conflict. They find nuclear war an intrinsically disproportionate means to any conceivable good end, and a means that renders the calculation of possible success meaningless. Nuclear pacifists also condemn nuclear deterrence. They hold that a state ought not to threaten explicitly or implicitly immoral acts (profound and sophisticated moralists such as John Bennett have been known to distinguish these propositions). Moreover, they hold that the possession of weapons systems, whose only logical function is to carry out immoral attacks, is itself immoral.

Authorities subscribing to these propositions tend to divide rather sharply into active pacifists and inactive dissenters. Pacifists such as Walter Stein, Justus George Lawler, and Gordon Zahn act through all means at their disposal, *e.g.,* writing, conferences, lobbying, to develop opposition to the policies of their governments which, in their view, are immoral. Other writers condemn nuclear war and deterrence in such a detached fashion that one hesitates to characterize them as pacifists. They give their moral diagnosis, condemn the whole basis for contemporary defense, and leave it to their readers to draw the practical conclusions.

One laudable characteristic of the activist pacifists is that they tend to meet the issue of the threat of Communist or other totalitarian aggression with a principled refusal to condone what they consider to be immoral means even to prevent a great evil from occurring. Admittedly, some nuclear pacifists are prone to play down the incompatibility between communism and Christianity. But some have gone so far as to map out programs of nonviolent resistance in the face of efforts by a Communist conqueror to interfere with freedom of conscience.

International Idealists. The broad term "international idealists" is applied here to those who urge abandonment of nuclear war and deterrence as well as other unilateral defense arrangements, relinquishment of national sovereignty and adhesion to a true international authority, which would eliminate war and rule over the world's people in peace and justice. Many proponents of this general position do not grapple with the problem of war in the way that pacifists do. They are more likely to emphasize the view that unilateral defense is outmoded and unnecessary, or will be if their blueprint is put into effect, than to maintain that the means of modern war are immoral and must never be used. Their object is the elimination rather than the management of force. To the extent that this is true, the international idealists remove themselves from our present discussion of morality and nuclear war and deterrence. The latter exists now, world government does not. The first question before us is, "What is the morality of the warlike preparations and activities in progress?" not, "What would life be like in a world where we would not have to make choices about the unilateral use of armed force?" The international idealists often fall short of the realism of the better pacifist thinkers in that they underestimate the profound character of the rift separating the Communist and non-Communist worlds, and, increasingly, the rifts within each bloc that do not appear to be amenable to efforts on behalf of international understanding.

Just War and Non-Combatant Immunity — Limited Nuclear War

In the sparse non-pacifist literature on morality and nuclear deterrence, the debate has remained centered on the traditional just war theory, both in its *jus ad bellum* and *jus in bello* aspects. The dominant themes that have emerged from this literature are:

(1) All the modern just war theorists who justify some kind of nuclear war and deterrence start with a grave concern over the threat of Communist aggression and the intrinsically anti-Christian character of any Communist *régime* that would be imposed on non-Communist victims of aggression. They tend to rate the necessity for nuclear defense and deterrence very high because they conceive of the threat as being extremely grave.

(2) Since "nuclear war and deterrence" may take many forms in many circumstances, it is improper to approve or condemn any such monolithic category of means.

(3) It is possible to envisage a use of nuclear weapons that would meet the conditions of proportionately grave cause: necessity, probable proportionality of good to evil effects, reasonable likelihood of success, respect for the principle of non-combatant

immunity from intentional direct attack and reasonable proportionality of ends to means. However, if *all* these conditions
are to be met, the number of imaginable licit uses of nuclear
weapons would seem to constitute a rather modest percentage of
any hypothetical total number of situations in which states might
maintain that military necessity required recourse to nuclear
weapons. Thus a moral conclusion justifying only such a comparatively limited use of nuclear weapons would be of academic
rather than practical importance. Such a position might have been
important in the early years of the nuclear age, but present-day
moral approval of such a limited nature would be comparatively
irrelevant.

(4) Just war theorists tend to accept the thesis that strategic or
general nuclear war, particularly counter-city war, is immoral but
that there is a level of limited nuclear war which can pass the test
imposed by the traditional just war conditions. In order to ac-
complish this, certain doctrinal and practical assumptions have
to be made.

In terms of *doctrine,* advocates of just limited nuclear war must
rely on the principle of double effect. Most of the forseeable uses
of limited nuclear war, *e.g.,* in defense of Europe or some parts
of the Far East, would take place in densely populated areas. If
one views the prospects for such a war without basing the analysis
on the double effect principle, it appears probable that many non-
combatants will inevitably be killed and injured as a result of the
employment of tactical or limited nuclear weapons. The same, of
course, can be said with respect to so-called conventional weapons.
Dependence upon the principle of double effect is essential to just
limited nuclear war theories, *if* the principle of non-combatant
immunity from intentional direct attack is to be respected.

In terms of practical assumptions, those who take the just
limited nuclear war position must assume at least two things:

(1) The dangers of escalation to an immoral level of general
nuclear war are not so great as to rule out the limited defense
ab initio on the grounds that the probable evil will outweigh the
probable good.

(2) There is a reasonable prospect of successful defense with
limited nuclear means *alone, i.e.,* there is a reasonable prospect of

success even though there is a nuclear threshold beyond which the just defender ought not and will not go.

Implicit in much of this literature, there is the assumption that the first use of nuclear weapons against superior conventional forces of an aggressor is justified. This assumption will not be examined at this point but the issue will be taken up in the final chapter.

The first assumption is precarious but barely tenable, given the terrible prospects of escalation of nuclear war. The second assumption is not tenable *unless* it rests on the basis of strategic nuclear deterrence. It is conceivable that a power deterred from strategic nuclear war will tacitly agree to conduct a limited nuclear war. It is hard to imagine a power which is not deterred at the strategic nuclear level participating in a limited nuclear war if the latter is disadvantageous. The price for limited nuclear defense appears to be the ability and willingness to mount a credible strategic nuclear deterrent and this, in turn, certainly requires a willingness to execute the strategic nuclear deterrent threat. Yet the very fact that some proponents of limited nuclear war embrace it as an *alternative* to what they have already designated as an immoral means, *i.e.,* strategic nuclear war, places them in a dilemma. They want to insure the defense of the Free World against Communist or other attack, but the limited nuclear war they specify as the outside limit of a morally permissible defense leaves them with a defense that may be moral but that is in all likelihood not sufficient.

If this analysis is correct, limited nuclear war might well be ruled out in most of the situations in which its use is presently contemplated, on the grounds of disproportionality and inadequate likelihood of success. For if a limited, and only a limited, nuclear defense of an area like Western Europe (supplemented, of course, by a conventional defense) is all that is morally permitted, even against a major nuclear power possessing both the ability and willingness to employ strategic nuclear weapons denied by moral scruples to the defenders, why should *any* defense be mounted? Why submit western Europe to the ravages of a limited nuclear-conventional defense and also risk the destruction of American and European cities through enemy employment of strategic nuclear weapons if there is little rational hope that the U.S. and its European allies could long hold up in such a disadvantageous situation? If common sense tells us that it is unlikely that even an enlightened state would stick to its moral scruples in a situation like this, why pretend that a limited nuclear war policy is an adequate, realistic defense policy, against a strategic deterrence policy? Whatever the prospects for independent limited nuclear war policies in the late fifties, it is clear that all major nuclear powers today, not to mention existing and potential minor nuclear powers, start with strategic nuclear deterrence as the foundation for their defense policies. It is in terms of a reconciliation of the requirements of the just war doctrine and strategic nuclear deterrence that the proponents of the former must find a justification for present U.S. and Western defense policies.

Just War and Non-Combatant Immunity —
Strategic Nuclear Deterrence

In the language of contemporary strategic doctrine, nuclear war is divided into "counter-force" and "counter-city" (also "counter-value") warfare. Given the enormous power and potential long-range effects of strategic nuclear weapons, the distinction is necessarily one in which the categories overlap. An attack on Washington or Moscow is clearly a counter-city attack. An attack on isolated missile sites in Montana or Siberia would be a counter-force attack. However, the so-called "collateral" damage to non-military targets and to non-combatants that may accompany a counter-force strike may be so devastating as to render the distinction tragically academic.

The just war theorist who insists on the continued validity of the principle of non-combatant immunity from intentional direct attack is therefore obliged to justify "collateral" damage from counter-force strikes under the principle of double effect if he is to support even a strictly counter-force execution of a deterrent threat. The pressure that this interpretation places upon the already heavily-burdened principle of double effect is probably greater than it can bear.

As an example, imagine one thousand nuclear devices in the megaton category exploded over Soviet missile sites, all of which are sufficiently removed from large population centers so that initial blast, firestorm and local radiological effects will not destroy such centers. There will be considerable loss of life of non-combatants in smaller population centers in the target areas but may this not be justified, as in the case of the use of indiscriminate projectiles against medieval fortresses, under the double effect interpretation that the intent is direct attack on and destruction of major military targets and that the destruction of non-combatants is incidental?

Even if this interpretation is accepted, there remains the problem of residual fall-out which, after such a large-scale attack would probably contaminate major population centers, even those at great distances from the military targets. We also know that the resultant fall-out from such an attack will probably have effects, according to geographic and climatic factors, all over the world. It seems rather a strained interpretation of the principle of double effect to call this potentially widespread lethal fall-out "accidental" and not directly "intended."

Any traditional just war justification for carrying out a strategic nuclear deterrent threat, if it is to hold to the principle of non-combatant immunity from intentional direct attack, will have to press to the limits the resources of the principle of double effect. To bring this off as justification for an outright counter-city attack would appear to be hopeless. To manage such a justification for large-scale counter-force attacks with substantial collateral damage seems extremely difficult.

Confronted with these problems, some advocates of the traditional just war theory have investigated the possibilities for maintaining strategic nuclear deterrents, the full use of which they concede to be immoral, in hopes that the threat implicit in the very existence of such nuclear deterrence systems would prevent their being challenged. Some moralists, anxious to avoid the stripping of Western defenses and the encouragement of Communist nuclear blackmail, advocate *a policy of maintaining the capability to do things which a just nation ought not and would not do*. Even if the West were to announce formally to the world that it would not conduct counter-city warfare, enemy leaders would presumably be extremely skeptical. Responsible enemies could not take much for granted. If the West in fact possessed a counter-city capability, how could enemy leaders be certain that, under the stress of nuclear attack, Christians might not abandon their principles? Or that others, not inclined to observe moral restraints, might not take over the governments in the West and change policy? Such a situation — having a counter-city capability but *not intending* to use it — could bring about the best of two worlds. Effective deterrence could perhaps be had together with a clean conscience about nuclear preparations. If this solution seems far-fetched, it can only be pointed out that some of the best minds attracted to the dilemmas of deterrence and morality have been driven to this approach.

Just War and Proportionality

There are at least two points of view that are not restricted by the traditional non-combatant immunity concept, but that are otherwise substantially in agreement with the just war theory. These are the positions of some of the so-called international realists (we refer here to morally concerned, not amoral, "realists"), most of whom are Protestants (Reinhold Niebuhr, Ernest W. Lefever, Robert Gessert, etc.), and some Catholic thinkers whose views on the perennial need for controlled use of force in some respects place them in the realist camp.

For the morally concerned realists, sinful human nature and the resultant primacy of power in politics render illusory the hopes of the international idealists for a world without "power politics" and war. They contend that all politics is "power politics" because purpose and power are inescapably involved. For them, the problem is one of limiting political objectives and choosing appropriate means, including a proportional measure of military coercion. For most of the realists, a pessimistic view of human nature leads to the opinion that the ultimate moral problem in politics is to minimize evil and to act responsibly so as to make the best of situations for which there will never be an ideal moral solution. Universal moral prescriptions such as prohibition of intentional direct attacks on noncombatants are, generally speaking, alien to this viewpoint. Emphasis is placed upon prudence and the principle of proportionality. The content of the latter principle has necessarily to be determined primarily on a case-by-case basis. Lasting codifications of the principle with respect to any particular means are considered neither possible nor desirable.

Applied to the problems of nuclear war and deterrence, the realist will reject any inflexible norm that threatens to preclude the effective defense of a state's rights. He will, instead feel the use of particular means in particular situations, *e.g.,* those used by Hitler in asserting Germany's claims, to be wrong. In assessing the means by which a state such as the United States defends itself and its allies, the realist will emphasize the need for prudent decision-makers backed by prudent citizens who in effect, are "doing their best" to limit foreign and defense policies to what is "necessary." In each practical situation the morally concerned "realist" asks: Are the goals morally justifiable? Are the means appropriate? He rejects as "impractical" abstract rules, whether moral or legal, that might interfere with policies which appear "reasonable" and morally justifiable.

An alternative but quite similar view is open to Catholics who accept the just war theory generally but who do not accept the non-combatant immunity principle without reservations. We have seen that the sticking point in all the debates over modern war has been the principle of non-combatant immunity from intentional direct attack. Because of respect for this principle the just war theorists have been driven to highly tenuous applications of the principle of double effect — or to the conclusion that nuclear war and deterrence (indeed, modern conventional war as well) exceed the limits of the just war theory. However, some writers, the author being one of them, remain unconvinced about the perennial, obligatory character of the non-combatant immunity principle as it has been generally interpreted. This view will be explained more fully in the concluding chapter. It is enough to identify here a viewpoint that, disagreeing with the antecedents of much of modern international realist thought, agrees with the latter's rejection of interpretations of the just war theory that condemn as immoral any really efficacious nuclear deterrence policy. This view would tend to part company with most of the international realists on the feasibility and desirability of building up mixed legal-moral rules of custom that would limit the options of the "responsible decision-maker" in his measured use of power. We shall return to this theme after an investigation of the work of Vatican Council II on the subject.

6
Vatican Council II:
Schema 13

The First Draft

In the fall of 1964, Vatican Council II turned briefly to the draft of what was to be the Council's last document, the *Pastoral Constitution on the Church in the Modern World* (at that point, Schema 17.) Article 25 of the Schema dealt with our subject matter. In order that fairness and independence of judgment be maximized it is suggested that the reader read carefully the text of the 1964 Draft Schema (Appendix A), bearing in mind the issues that have emerged from our discussion, before proceeding with the analysis that follows.

The salient points in the draft Schema appear to be the following:

(1) The terrible nature of "new weapons capable of destroying the entire human family" is stressed. Abhorrence of these weapons permeates the text.

(2) While the balance of terror is not explicitly dealt with, the Schema emphasizes that the world has "no true peace." The blame for this absence of peace is placed on the "weapons of spreading terror" that are "opposed to peace."

(3) The right of legitimate self-defense is barely and reluctantly acknowledged, *viz.,* "Although, after all the aids of peaceful discussion have been exhausted, it may not be illicit, when one's rights have been unjustly hampered, to defend those rights against such aggression by violence and force; nevertheless, the use of arms, especially nuclear weapons, whose effects are greater than

can be imagined and therefore cannot be reasonably regulated by men, exceeds all just proportion and therefore must be judged before God and man as most wicked. . . ."

(4) From the latter part of the foregoing quotation, we may infer that, recalling Pius XII's formulation, any means, whether nuclear or not, which escape human control are immoral because they exceed any conceivable "just proportion."

(5) War as "an instrument suited for the redressing of violated rights" is "becoming ever more absurd" for two reasons; one negative and the other positive:

(a) "Since the terrifying destructive force, which is daily increasing in war arms, is able to cause calamities and horrible destruction throughout the world . . ."

(b) ". . . since technological progress, communications and organizations for peacefully settling disputes are daily proving more effective . . ."

It is important to break down this complex sentence into its major elements. The language seems to indicate that offensive war to "redress" violated rights is "ever more absurd." But is such a war prohibited, as Pius XII held? The statement is unclear. When we turn to the two reasons supporting the conclusion we find considerable room for criticism and controversy. Most commentators would agree with the first, negative reason. The presumption is certainly against nuclear war as either a means of protecting rights or of redressing violated rights. The second reason, which is also rather vague, is highly controversial. At the time this draft was being produced, conflict persisted in dozens of places all over the world, *e.g.,* Cyprus, Malaysia, Vietnam, the Congo, India. Each of these conflicts revealed again the modest ability of the institutions of international law and organization to prevent, contain, or end them.

(6) Calling for an end to the arms race, the draft Schema states: "Therefore the Sacred Council denounces as a ruinous injury inflicted upon the whole human family, and in severest terms censures the uncontrollable armaments race, inasmuch as it is injurious to and prevents real peace, harmony and trust among nations, places a great part of mankind in danger of their lives, and dissipates the wealth needed for much better things." The rulers

of the world are called upon "to deliver their people from this danger by agreements which will effectively work out a just peace and at the same time they must endeavor to put out of men's minds all hostility, hatred and mistrust. Better aids must be chosen to prevent wars and peacefully remove conflicts; among these aids are the following: consistent progress in building up a universal community among the nations, all of which will remain free; an international authority having at its disposal the means necessary to avoid war and to promote peace, so as to bring about conditions in which war of any kind can no longer be regarded as a legitimate instrument, even for the defense of one's own rights."

In terms of the issues that we have been examining, let us analyze the 1964 draft Schema. First, it reflected an idealist view that war and preparations for war are not only evil but tragically *unnecessary*. The origins of international conflict generally or the particular sources of contemporary conflict, *e.g.,* communism, the revolution of former colonial peoples, racial hatred etc., are not dealt with. Yet at the very time when the draft was produced, all sorts of conflicts raged that did not result primarily from any arms race or the existence of weapons but from other deep-rooted causes.

Second, the draft Schema also reflected an idealist view that the true goal of international morality, law, and organization is the complete elimination of international conflict and of the weapons of war. It did not grapple with the implications of man's sinfulness or our historical experience with both domestic and international politics for this point of view. Neither did it deal with the fact that modern weapons and delivery systems cannot be "uninvented" and that, therefore, even a world state would face problems of preventing and winning conflicts waged in defiance of international law and order.

Third, although the draft Schema conceded the right of self-defense, it left unanswered most of the questions concerned with permissible and impermissible forms of self-defense.

Fourth, it did not explicitly confront the problem of nuclear deterrence either as the basis for what little peace and order exists in the world or as the logical requirement of a posture of legitimate self-defense *vis-à-vis* a potential nuclear aggressor. The draft

Schema did, however, "censure the uncontrollable arms race" and thereby presumably, those nations engaged in it, without any distinction as to the reasons for their participation.

This writer is highly critical of the original draft of Sehema 13's Article 25. His dissatisfaction arose not only from disagreement with some of the conclusions of the draft and from its tone of righteous condemnation but from its incompleteness, vagueness, and failure to come to grips with the implications of its moral conclusions. If a document is to "censure" something as important and complex as the contemporary arms race and nuclear deterrence system, it should be complete, explicit, and responsible. In this writer's opinion the document was deficient in all three respects. Fortunately, a thorough revision of it was made and submitted to the Council.

Schema 13 Revised — the Pastoral Constitution
On the Church in the Modern World

The reader would do well to read carefully Chapter V of the *Pastoral Constitution on the Church in the Modern World,* the revised version of that part of Schema 13 that deals with nuclear war (Appendix B). The analysis that follows will sometimes depart from the sequence in which subjects are dealt with in the Constitution in order that the general line of analysis followed in this book may be maintained.

The final version of Schema 13 which the Council Fathers accepted is, from a just war point of view, a marked improvement over the original draft presented in 1964. Although Article 25 emphasizes the need for "true peace," it acknowledges the perennial character of war and, therefore, of the right of self-defense (or of its replacement by an effective international security system). Although the Council condemned "the frightfulness of war" it stated clearly:

> Insofar as men are sinners, the threat of war hangs over them and will so continue until the coming of Christ; but insofar as they can vanquish sin by coming together in

charity, violence itself will be vanquished and they will make these words come true: "They shall beat their swords into ploughshares, and their spears into pruning hooks; nation shall not lift up sword against nation, neither shall they learn war any more" (Is. 2,4). (*Pastoral Constitution on the Church in the Modern World,* Art. 78.)

On the basis of this judgment, which is at the heart of the traditional just war theory, the Council reasserts the right of legitimate self-defense:

> War, of course, has not ceased to be part of the human scene. As long as the danger of war persists and there is no international authority with the necessary competence and power, governments cannot be denied the right of lawful self-defense, once all peace efforts have failed. (*Ibid.,* Art. 79.)

The conditions of true necessity, of right intention, and of limitation of means are added immediately to that of exhaustion of peaceful remedies:

> State leaders and all who share the burdens of public administration have the duty to defend the interest of their people and to conduct such grave matters with a deep sense of responsibility. However, it is one thing to wage a war of self-defense; it is quite another to seek to impose domination on another nation . . . Nor does the mere fact that war has unfortunately broken out mean that all is fair between the warring parties. (*Ibid.,* Art. 79)

Having seen that the Council reaffirmed the *jus ad bellum* elements of the just war theory, let us concentrate now on its treatment of the morality of modern means of warfare. The first point to be stressed is the insistence of the Constitution that "the natural law of peoples and its universal principles still retain their binding force." Clearly, whatever is held to violate these principles cannot be justified, even by the allegation of the highest necessities of state. The Council said: "Any action which deliberately violates these principles and any order which commands such actions is criminal and blind obedience cannot excuse those who carry them out." What then, are the relevant principles of the universal natural law?

The first principle is that prohibiting genocide. The Council did not use the word, but the crime it describes is that of genocide. The Constitution states: "The most infamous among these actions [conflicting with the natural law] are those designed for the reasoned and methodical extermination of an entire race, nation, or ethnic minority. These must be condemned as frightful crimes; and we cannot commend too highly the courage of the men who openly and fearlessly resist those who issue orders of this kind." (*Ibid.,* Art. 79)

Having referred to natural law principles and identified one of them, the Constitution then moves to related matters but does not identify other principles in the way that it prohibited genocide. It refers, rather, to the positive international law of war, stating:

> On the question of warfare, there are various international conventions, signed by many countries, aimed at rendering military action and its consequences less inhuman; they deal with the treatment of wounded and interned prisoners of war and with various kindred questions. These agreements must be preserved; indeed public authorities and specialists in these matters must do all in their power to improve these conventions and thus bring about a better and more effective curbing of the savagery of war. (*Ibid.,* Art. 79)

To those who have seen the laws of war scorned, neglected, even condemned as subversive to the true search for peace, this reference is most heartening. Among other things it reaffirms the conviction of the Council that war is going to be with us for a long time and that there are things that can and ought to be done to limit its effects.

There then follows a most interesting series of points. First, in the last sentence of the paragraph just quoted, the Council observes that "it seems just that humane laws should regulate the case of conscientious objectors who refuse to carry arms, provided some other form of community service is substituted." (*Ibid.,* Art. 79)

This reverses the position that the Church, notably in the explicit language of Pius XII, had taken on conscientious objection.

Second, the Constitution reiterates the right of self-defense already quoted. Thirdly, in the last brief paragraph of Article 79, the Constitution, in effect, balances its nod in the direction of conscientious objection with a tribute to the military, stating:

> All those who enter the military service in loyalty to their country should look upon themselves as the custodians of the security and freedom of their fellow-countrymen; and when they carry out their duty properly, they are contributing to the maintenance of peace. (*Ibid.,* Art. 79)

Particularly in contrast to the "curse on both your houses" tone of the original Schema 13's "censure" of the participants in the arms race, these passages of Article 79 stand out as strong reaffirmation of the rights and duties of just defense.

The Constitution moves, in Article 80, to a more specific examination of modern war and adds two more principles, presumably "natural law principles," to its guidelines on war and morality. One prohibits "total war," and the second prohibits indiscriminate counter-city warfare. With respect to the first, the Constitution says:

> The development of armaments by modern science has immeasurably magnified the horrors and wickedness of war. Warfare conducted with these weapons can inflict immense and indiscriminate havoc which goes far beyond the bounds of legitimate defense. Indeed if the kind of weapons now stocked in the arsenals of the great powers were to be employed to the fullest, the result would only be the almost complete reciprocal slaughter of one side by the other, not to speak of the widespread devastation that would follow in the world and the deadly after-effects resulting from the use of such arms.
>
> All these factors force us to undertake a completely fresh reappraisal of war. Men of this generation should realize that they will have to render an account of their warlike behavior; the destiny of generations to come depends largely on the decisions they make today.

With these considerations in mind the Council, endorsing

the condemnations of total warfare issued by recent popes
. . . (*Ibid.,* Art. 80)

This is clearly a condemnation of general nuclear war and
apparently also embraces World War II forms of "total war." At
this point no hint is given as to the rights of a just defender
attacked by an aggressor using such means.

With respect to the second prohibition the Constitution states
flatly:

> Every act of war directed to the indiscriminate destruction
> of whole cities or vast areas with their inhabitants is a crime
> against God and man, which merits firm and unequivocal
> condemnation. (*Ibid.,* Art. 80)

The rationale for this statement is not given. We are not told
whether it is based on the principle of non-combatant immunity
from intentional, direct attack or on the principle of proportionality or both. Nevertheless, it is an explicit and powerful judgment
that counter-city warfare is immoral.

The Constitution then returns to the theme of the uniqueness of
modern war and, in turn, of nuclear deterrence, and of the need
for "entirely new" attitudes toward them.

First, in a welcome paragraph, the Constitution recognizes that
the object of a realistic inquiry into the morality of nuclear war
and deterrence is a weapons *system* and not "the bomb" or even
"nuclear war." It observes:

> The hazards peculiar to modern warfare consist in the
> fact that they expose those possessing recently developed
> weapons to the risk of perpetuating crimes like these and,
> by an inexorable chain of events, of urging men to even
> worse acts of atrocity. To obviate the possibility of this
> happening at any time in the future, the bishops of the world
> gathered together implore all men, especially government
> leaders and military advisors, to give unceasing consideration
> to their immense responsibilities before God and before the
> whole human race. (*Ibid.,* Art, 80)

Second, in Article 81, the Constitution treats of nuclear
deterrence, saying:

Undoubtedly, armaments are not amassed merely for use in wartime. Since the defensive strength of any nation is thought to depend on its capacity of immediate retaliation, the stockpiling of arms which grows from year to year, serves, in a way hitherto unthought of, as a deterrent to potential attackers. Many people look upon this as the most effective way known at the present time for maintaining some sort of peace among nations.

Whatever one may think of this form of deterrent, people are convinced that the arms race, which quite a few countries have entered, is no infallible way for maintaining real peace and that the resulting so-called balance of power is no sure and genuine path to achieving it. Rather than eliminate the causes of war, the arms race serves only to aggravate the position. As long as extravagant sums of money are poured into the development of new weapons, it is impossible to devote adequate aid to tackling the misery which prevails at the present day in the world. Instead of eradicating international conflict once and for all, the contagion is spreading to other parts of the world. New approaches, based on a renewal of mentality, will have to be chosen in order to remove this stumbling-block, to free the earth from its pressing anxieties, and give back to the world a genuine peace. (*Ibid.*, Art. 81)

Three conclusions are reasonably clear from this treatment of deterrence:

(1) Despite the preceding unequivocal condemnation of counter-city warfare the Council did not condemn strategic nuclear deterrence which at present rests in large measure upon the credible threat to retaliate in kind to a nuclear attack.

(2) The Constitution leaves open the question of the morality and prudence of reliance on nuclear deterrence, notably in the noncommittal words, "Many people look upon this as the most effective way known at the present time," and the opening phrase of the first sentence in the paragraph immediately following, *viz.,* "Whatever one may think of this form of deterrent . . ."

(3) Like *Pacem in Terris,* the Constitution is more concerned with inducing positive action than in condemnations, censures and recriminations. The words "New approaches, based on a renewal of mentality, will have to be chosen in order to remove this stumbling-block, to free the earth from its pressing anxieties, and give back to the world a genuine peace" constitute more than an

inspiring call to action. They convey a moral imperative as binding and important as any negative prohibition that the Council may have laid down.

The last conclusion is supported by the reiteration of the Council's call to action:

> Therefore, we declare once again: the arms race is one of the greatest curses on the human race and the harm it inflicts on the poor is more than can be endured. And there is every reason to fear that if it continues it will bring forth those lethal disasters which are already in preparation. Warned by the possibility of the catastrophes that man has created let us profit by the respite we now enjoy, thanks to divine favor, to take stock of our responsibilities and find ways of resolving controversies in a manner more worthy of human beings. Providence urgently demands of us that we free ourselves from the age-old slavery of war. If we refuse to make this effort, there is no knowing where we will be led on the fatal path we have taken. (*Ibid.,* Art. 81)

The Constitution then specifies the goals and the approaches to them that seem most productive. The goals are:

(1) A universal public authority;

(2) Interim measures to achieve common security and a true beginning of disarmament.

Of the world public authority the Constitution says:

> It is our clear duty to spare no effort in order to work for the moment when all war will be completely outlawed by international agreement. This goal, of course, requires the establishment of a universally acknowledged public authority vested with the effective power to ensure security for all, regard for justice, and respect for law. (*Ibid.,* Art. 82)

Recognizing that such an authority is not presently foreseeable, the Constitution then observes:

> But before this desirable authority can be constituted, it is necessary for existing international bodies to devote themselves resolutely to the exploration of better means for obtaining common security. But since peace must be born of mutual trust between peoples instead of being forced on na-

tions through dread of arms, all must work to put an end to
the arms race and make a real beginning of disarmament,
not unilaterally indeed but at an equal rate on all sides, on
the basis of agreements and backed up by genuine and effective guarantees. (*Ibid.,* Art. 82)

It is edifying to discern in this appeal a fair and realistic disa-
vowal of unilateral disarmament and a recognition of the requirements for disarmament arrangements in a world that is still
divided by deep-rooted antagonisms and distrust.

When the Constitution turns from the goals of international law,
order, and disarmament to the means of attaining those goals, it
emphasizes the following:

(1) We should respect and support "efforts already made or
now underway to eliminate the danger of war" and which "are not
to be underestimated." Again, here is a welcome shift in emphasis
from generalized condemnation of war to support for practical
efforts to solve the problem of war. Specifically, the Constitution
refers to international meetings and studies which "are to be
considered as the first steps toward the solutions of such important
questions and must be further pursued with even greater insistence,
with a view to obtaining concrete results in the future." (*Ibid.,*
Art. 82)

(2) We should contribute to building public opinion in support
of enlightened efforts for international law, order, and disarmament. The efforts of the few peacemakers will be in vain "as long
as men are divided and warring among themselves through
hostility, contempt, and distrust, as well as through racial hatred
and uncompromising hostilities." The Constitution then continues:

. . . Hence there is a very urgent need of re-education and
renewed orientation of public opinion. Those engaged in the
work of education, especially youth education, and the people
who mold public opinion, should regard it as their most
important task to educate the minds of men to renewed sentiments of peace. Every one of us needs a change of heart; we
must set our gaze on the whole world and look to those
tasks we can all perform together in order to bring about the
betterment of our race. (*Ibid.,* Art. 82)

(3) In addition to related efforts to strengthen international institutions and cooperation (see Articles 83-88), the Constitution singles out one further means for reaching the ends relating to the avoidance of war. Article 90 of the Constitution calls for increased studies, meetings, and dialogues by and between institutes and associations concerned with international problems. It says:

> For Christians one undoubtedly excellent form of international activity is the part they play, either individually or collectively, in organizations set up or on the way to being set up to foster cooperation between nations. Different Catholic international bodies can assist the community of nations on the way to peace and brotherhood; these bodies should be strengthened by enlarging the number of their well-trained members, by increasing the subsidies they need so badly, and by suitable coordination of their forces. Nowadays efficiency of action and the need for dialogue call for initiatives in common. Organizations of this kind, moreover, contribute more than a little to the instilling of a feeling of universality, which is certainly appropriate for Catholics, and to the formation of truly world-wide solidarity and responsibility. (*Ibid.,* Art. 90)

The Constitution adds that this kind of activity should where appropriate be carried on in cooperation with our "separated brethren, who profess the charity of the Gospel along with [us], and also with all men thirsting for true peace." (*Ibid.*, Art. 90)

With the *Pastoral Constitution,* papal teaching and the views of just war theorists in mind, let us now apply the principles of modern just war doctrine to the defense policies of the United States and its allies.

7

The Just War Theory and
U.S. Defense Policies

Defense policies in the United States remain the basis for the defense of the Free World. As far as the use of nuclear weapons is concerned they may be summarized as follows:

(1) The United States has pledged that it will never initiate a war of any kind. If this pledge is kept, U.S. policies will conform to modern prescription against offensive just wars.

(2) Under the flexible response concept, the U.S. claims the right and asserts that it has the capability to respond to an aggressive attack on itself or its allies with means proportionate to the requirements of a successful defense. This capability and disposition is regarded as a deterrent to an enemy first strike.

(3) The U.S. has refrained from promising that it would never use nuclear weapons first. It reserves the right to use them in cases of grave and flagrant aggression where available conventional means of defense are inadequate. One may infer from official U.S. attitudes that there is a conviction that ambiguity on this point has a salutary effect on potential aggressors, *i.e.,* ambiguity adds to effective deterrence.

The most critical aspect of the issue of first use of nuclears is raised by the integration of hundreds of tactical nuclear weapons in the NATO forces defending Western Europe. It is difficult to imagine these weapons being withheld from combat in the event of a major attack by Communist conventional forces. (Although one must recognize the efforts of the United States to ensure control of these weapons.)

(4) The U.S. has emphasized that its *preferred* strategy is to

avoid nuclear war and minimize the scale of any nuclear war in which it might become engaged. Specifically with respect to cities, U.S. policy is to seek to limit nuclear war to counter-force strikes, reserving counter-city warfare for possible retaliation in kind as part of what McNamara has called "assured destruction" measures, *i.e.,* the purpose of retaliatory counter-city strikes would be to deter further attacks on American cities rather than blind revenge.

(5) The U.S. believes that credible strategic nuclear deterrence is absolutely indispensable, not only to the defense of the Free World but to the maintenance of minimum world public order in an age of continuing conflict and possible nuclear proliferation. The *sine qua non* of this deterrent is the continued *certainty* in the minds of all nations that the deterrent threat *will* be executed if the deterrent is gravely challenged by an aggressor.

(6) The U.S. proposals for a three-stage general and complete disarmament start with the assumption that any such advances must: (1) begin with a mutual stable deterrence balance between the major powers; (2) proceed by way of fairly balanced mutual scaling down of the deterrent and defense forces until the problem of deterrence and maintenance of international law and order can be assumed by a world authority.

The Modern Just War: "jus ad bellum"

If we apply the conditions for just war as they have been reiterated, and in some cases revised, by the recent popes and Vatican Council II we might come to the following conclusions:

(1) *Just Cause.* Pope Pius XII's words after the Hungarian revolt should be recalled as we judge the necessity of defense against Communist and other totalitarian aggression. The maintenance of the U.S. deterrent and defense forces is not a result of selfish power politics nor of excessive nationalism. Rather it is a result of the dangerous world conditions with which the United States must cope. Sufficient cause for a nuclear war would have to be extraordinarily grave. Despite U.S. ambiguity on this point, the only cause sufficient to justify a nuclear war would be a prior

nuclear attack by an aggressor or an immediate, certain, clear and present danger of such an attack. That this has been recognized by the U.S. is proven by the fact that the only particular, explicit threat of nuclear war (as distinguished from the continued, generalized deterrent threat) ever made by this country was that made by President Kennedy in his October 22, 1962 Cuban Missile Crisis speech. The threat was retaliation in kind for Soviet or Cuban missile attacks on the United States.

As to the proportionality of a nuclear war — even a limited one — and the probability of success, it is significant that the United States has never engaged in such a war and, as far as can be ascertained, has never seriously contemplated initiation of a nuclear war. What we know of suggestions to use nuclear weapons in defense of Dien Bien Phu in 1954 and elsewhere seems to place advocates of their use in a distinct minority insofar as responsible decision-makers are concerned.

A word should be said about the requirement that peaceful remedies be exhausted before an aggrieved party undertakes a just war. This condition should always be interpreted in the context of the ideological conflicts that dominate the world scene. Courts of law apply the term "justiciable" to legal controversies which can be settled in a court. The basic issues underlying contemporary international conflict are essentially non-justiciable.

A controversy such as the Indian-Pakistani dispute over Kashmir would be justiciable in the International Court of Justice or in a special arbitral tribunal. Only the nationalistic enmities of the parties prevent this. But how "settle" a controversy over, for example, alleged indirect aggression in the form of the external organization, direction, and support of a revolutionary civil war in a target state? Whether the external aggressor is Communist, an advocate of some regional or racial "pan" movement, or even Western, it has no dispute with the target state in the sense of the Kashmir dispute. It has, rather, a profound ideological conviction that the social system in the target state is bad, that it is inevitably destined to be replaced by the social system of the aggressor, and that therefore, it is right to organize a war which will tear the target state apart. Such a "controversy" can be settled only by force of arms — unless one or more of the parties changes its fundamental assumptions or loses its will to carry them to their logical conclusion.

With respect to essentially non-justiciable controversies, the condition of "exhaustion of peaceful remedies" should be interpreted primarily in a diplomatic-political rather than legal sense. Negotiations, directly or through intermediaries, use of the organs of the United Nations and of regional organizations, establishment of international inspection and peacekeeping units, are the peaceful remedies that must be used. However, as the Cuban Missile Crisis demonstrated, the definition of "full use" of such measures is more a function of the characteristics of the situation than of the expiration of time or the number and variety of peaceful means that are tried.

(2) *Right Intention.* There is a great deal of fear and hatred in the world. A substantial amount of it is directed against the United States. Hatred begets more hatred. This natural psychological phenomenon must be overcome by Christians and all men of good will. No matter what the provocation, defense and deterrence policies must be conceived and carried out in a spirit of charity. No amount of injustice in the attitudes and behavior of actual or potential opponents can justify a departure on the part of national decision-makers and citizens from the requirement of right intention in a just war. If outraged consciences require more than this moral imperative to control them, it would be well to review developments during and after World War II. Within a few years, the Japanese and Germans who had been conceived of as evil incarnate were the most reliable friends of the United States, and some wartime allies whose "image" had been romanticized during the war were increasingly cast in the role of villains.

First Use of Nuclear Weapons

We have noted the fact that NATO defense plans and arrangements presently result in a mixed limited nuclear-conventional defense. Consequently there is the possibility of some kind of limited nuclear and conventional war in defense of Western Europe. Alternatively it is conceivable that an aggressor might be met with conventional means only. What are the implications, insofar as these defense arrangements are concerned, of contemporary just war statements by the Church?

The answer is extremely difficult. Papal and conciliar guidelines prohibit "total war," war with means that "escape human control," and counter-city strikes. If we interpret "total war" in terms of its historic meaning in World War II, even a conventional defense of Western Europe would seem to be excluded. It is difficult to believe that this is the case. The firm reiteration of the right of legitimate self-defense appears to justify conventional defense of Western Europe if that defense did not involve indiscriminate conventional aerial attacks on population centers, and the kinds of crimes against humanity that characterized World War II.

As to limited nuclear war we can only say the following:

(1) Obviously there are forms of limited nuclear war that do not amount to the proscribed "total war" or weapons that "escape" human control.

(2) Such limited nuclear war measures are subject to the principle of non-combatant immunity from intentional, direct attack and to the general principle of proportionality. We shall leave the issue of the present status and meaning of non-combatant immunity to the next section. But it is clear that there are many possible uses for limited nuclear weapons which would not violate non-combatant rights or the principle of proportionality, *e.g.,* a one-kiloton device exploded against the staging area for an armored attack in an area from which all known refugees had been evacuated.

(3) If it be granted that some licit recourse to limited nuclear means is conceivable, what of widespread use of tactical nuclear weapons in prolonged combat waged in heavily populated Western Europe where destruction of non-combatant lives and property and contamination resulting from local fall-out would be unavoidable? Admittedly this question is difficult to grapple with because of serious doubts about its realism. Would the NATO nations choose such a form of defense which would probably wreck their homelands? On the other hand, this is the war that NATO is prepared to fight — unless it is believed that strategic nuclear deterrence aimed at the Communist bloc will in fact

prevent such a war. In the event that it does not, such a war would be superfluous since the real war will take the form of a nuclear show-down between the United States and the Soviet Union.

In any event, the permissibility of such a large scale "limited" nuclear-conventional defense of Europe (or any other area containing large numbers of civilian population centers) would appear to depend on how strictly or loosely one interprets the non-combatant immunity principle and the Council's prohibition of counter-city warfare. A strict interpretation would make effective defense very difficult. To the extent that the aggressor would be able to recognize the limitations that were being observed, he could easily protect himself by making it a point to operate as much as possible from civilian population centers and could even herd civilian hostages along with him. If the right of self-defense has any practical meaning, it is hard to accept interpretations of the Church's *jus in bello* that might produce such ludicrous situations. Has modern weapons technology rendered the right of self-defense morally irrelevant?

(4) Even if the foregoing problems can be surmounted, there remains the issue of the morality of *first use* of nuclear weapons. If one totals up the possible objections to tactical nuclear weapons, and then adds a more pessimistic estimate of the dangers of escalation, the presumptions are against such a war satisfying the condition of proportionality of probable evil and good effects. Of course one could posit circumstances in which the danger of escalation would not be disproportionate to the ends defended and the necessity for using limited nuclear means. But even such hypothetical just limited nuclear wars would face a further, more basic objection.

No nuclear device has been used in war since the Nagasaki bomb. Explicit threats to use nuclear weapons in particular situations have been extremely rare during more than twenty years of widespread international conflict in which just about everything else has been threatened and done. The universal practice of nuclear powers has been to hold nuclear weapons apart from their other arms and to reserve them for use to execute deterrent threats against possible nuclear attackers. In the language of international law, there has developed a "usage" against the first use of nuclear weapons. A usage is a pattern of behavior that has recurred sufficiently to be thought of as the normal or expected behavior with respect to a particular aspect of international relations. If and when the recurrence of the usage appears to be accompanied by a conviction that the normal pattern of behavior should be followed as an international legal obligation rather than as a habit, customary international law has been created.

Aside from the dangers of escalation, the first use of even very limited nuclear weapons would break the pattern of behavior with respect to first use of nuclear means which has survived unbroken since 1945. Pandora's box would be open — the breaking of the tacit ban on the first use of nuclear weapons would be a sorry event. It would be a hard saying to maintain that this event would never under any circumstances be justified, but certainly it is one that may increasingly attract the support of morally responsible persons in all nations.

This is a subject that is still open and that obviously requires intensive study and discussion. It affects the traditional heartland of Christendom. It is, moreover, one of the subjects about which something can be done. There is no sufficient reason why the defense of Western Europe and other parts of the Free World by conventional means cannot be assured. Alternatively, it may well become possible to lessen the already diminished threat of a general war in Europe by enlightened settlement of the problems of German reunification, the creation of nuclear free zones in Central Europe and the like. These goals are difficult but not visionary.

If present arrangements are continued and someday NATO finds itself in a position where it must break the tacit agreement prohibiting initiation of nuclear war, a heavy moral responsibility will rest upon all of us who have had some part, positively or negatively, in perpetuating a system that would foreseeably lead to such a result.

Strategic Nuclear Deterrence

If the modern teaching of the Church on just war were as clear as U.S. defense doctrine, it is likely that there would be a head-on collision between the two. American Catholics who wanted to be both good Americans and good Catholics would suffer from that collision. The teaching of the Church on this subject is still sufficiently vague and incomplete so that such a collision is not immediately imminent. But no one who wants to avoid a collision without participating in hypocricy and deception should have any doubt about the urgency of the problem of determining the moral limits of just defense and deterrence.

A word should be said here about the binding character of the papal statements and the *Pastoral Constitution on the Church in the Modern World*. It is clear that none of the principles and rules which we have been discussing must be accepted as binding in conscience. If we have valid and sufficient reasons, we may reject this moral guidance on matters of this kind. Thus a Catholic pacifist is free to pursue his convictions regardless of the reaffirmation even in the nuclear age of the rights and duties of just defense by the popes and the Council. But if a Catholic finds reason not to follow the social teaching of the Church, he cannot therefore disregard it.

With this grave problem in mind, let us recapitulate the main principles of the Church's modern just war *jus in bello:*

(1) Total war, war with means that escape man's control, genocide and counter-city war are all prohibited.

(2) Disproportionate means are prohibited.

(3) Direct, intentional killing of non-combatants is prohibited. This recapitulation attempts to combine the principles of the traditional just war theory which have not been changed or disavowed with the new, partly overlapping principles laid down by the popes and/or Vatican Council II in response to the challenges of modern war. We might begin with the assumption that all these principles are equally valid and persuasive to a reasonable man who takes seriously the sources from whence they came.

The writer is prepared to agree to this assumption with respect to the first two categories but not the third. Accordingly he must begin with the third principle. The reasons against accepting the principle of non-combatant immunity from direct intentional attack include:

(1) The principle is not clearly and explicitly present in the just war literature until the 16th and 17th centuries. It is not a self-evident principle of the natural law but a customary principle produced in municipal and international law which was incorporated into the just law doctrine.

(2) The incorporation of the principle of non-combatant immunity into the just war theory was justified because it was consistent with legitimate military necesssity at the time.

(3) Although many treatments of the subject by scholars and publicists continue to emphasize the principle, there is not a single explicit reference to it in the principal papal and conciliar statements on nuclear war. The principle is not mentioned as a rationale supporting the principles referred to in categories (1) and (2) above.

(4) In contrast to the state of military technology and science when the customary law principle of non-combatant immunity was introduced, continued application of the principle in its strict form (including the concept of "intent" herein rejected) would not only preclude most forseeable nuclear wars, but also almost any conceivable type of major defensive war in populated portions of the earth.

(5) The sources on which we have drawn reiterate the continued validity of the right of self-defense. The presumption must be that the authors quoted intended that right to be meaningful. But literal application of the traditional principle of non-combatant immunity would make major defensive wars impossible and render empty and illusory the right of self-defense.

(6) Efforts to solve the problem by designating virtually all of the enemy's population as participants in the war effort and hence not non-combatants will continue to be in vain. No matter what criteria are used, a considerable number of the enemy population are non-combatants and they will inevitably fall victim to the fate of the rest in major nuclear war.

(7) Efforts to solve the dilemma by justifying "unintended, indirect" attacks on non-combatants under the principle of double effect have been unsatisfactory and will become more so. When a belligerent unleashes many large nuclear weapons, even though they be directed at military targets, the inevitable result will be

death, injury and contamination for large numbers of non-combatants. To borrow from Professor Tucker's forthcoming book,* these non-combatant deaths may not be *desired* but they are certainly *intended*. To pretend otherwise is to add neither higher morality, clarity, or dignity to an attempt to meet our moral dilemmas.

This judgment is limited to the issue of non-combatant immunity. The author has neither the desire nor the competence to evaluate the validity and usefulness of the principle of double effect generally. But he does contend that in the context of modern war and deterrence, it does not furnish a tool of normative analysis that is morally, rationally, and psychologically satisfactory. It simply does not ring true.

For these reasons, from the viewpoint of those attempting to wage just defensive war today, it is necessary and proper to question non-combatant immunity as an absolute principle. The concept of non-combatant immunity from direct intentional attack is certainly a preferred goal, a guideline to belligerents, which they are morally obliged to respect. But it may be questioned whether non-combatant immunity as an absolute principle is compatible with the exercise of the legitimate rights of defense which Catholic social teaching has so often and so recently reiterated. Given the state of military technology, strategy and tactics, modern war is characterized at every level by the military necessity of taking measures that will inevitably involve death and injury to non-combatants no matter what the "intent" of the belligerents.

At this point critics of modern just war positions generally charge that morality is being made sudordinate to the arbitrary demands of militarists and the inhuman exigencies of military technology. This is not necessarily the case. Any practical moral analysis has to confront the material "given" of the subject mater, *e.g.,* the facts of human reproduction, the economics of development, or the social attitudes of victims of discrimination. The material facts relevant to the subject of morality and war are the facts about the requirements for mounting a successful military defense in the modern world. If on their face these requirements

* Robert W. Tucker and Robert Osgood, *Force, Order and Justice* (Baltimore: The Johns Hopkins Press, 1967).

contravene absolute moral principles there can be no moral defense. But the Church, well aware of the character of modern war, has confirmed the continued existence of the right of defense. We are left, therefore, with the question whether the good of saving one's society through legitimate defense is in some circumstances sufficient reason for the killing of non-combatants which must inevitably accompany such defense.

Once this question is settled, a morally permissible just defense and deterrence theory may be possible. There are still difficulties but such a just defense is at least conceivable. Virtually no just defense is conceivable if the traditional non-combatant immunity principle is binding.

What are the outstanding difficulties of reconciling present Western nuclear deterrence policies and the modern just war theory of the Church? The central difficulty has to do with retaliation in kind. It seems clear that the United States has no desire or rational need to initiate "total war," or war with means escaping human control. It certainly has no disposition to engage in genocide, *i.e.,* systematic destruction of a people because of ideological, racial or other reasons unrelated to military necessity. We have seen that it is U.S. policy not to attack population centers, except as retaliation in kind to prevent further destruction to American or allied cities.

Here we have the heart of the problem. U.S. strategic deterrence presently rests upon a credible willingness to respond to nuclear attacks with an ascending scale of retaliatory strikes. The character of those strikes would presumably be determined by a calculation as to the kinds and amounts of nuclear force necessary first, to deter the enemy from continuing his attacks, and second, to limit further damage as much as possible by reducing his offensive nuclear capabilities. The "intent" or, to use Tucker's term, "desire" of the United States would be essentially to wage counter-force warfare. But the calculus of retaliation is in large measure determined by the means employed by the nuclear aggressor. Hence no strategy based primarily on proportionality of means to the just ends of self-defense can set a limit for itself that does not exceed the limits set by the *Pastoral Constitution on the Church in the Modern World*.

Thus the imposition of a rigid "no cities" (as distinguished from "no first attack on cities") rule raises the spectre of nuclear blackmail by a belligerent disinclined to accept any limits. However, as Ramsey and others have suggested, there may be an escape from this dilemma. We have seen that even so-called counter-force strikes are likely to have devastating effects on an enemy society. Even if it were possible to carry out many counter-force strikes against more-or-less isolated military targets without excessive direct damage to non-combatants, the long range effects of the fall-out from such strikes alone would presumably be very great. Would the threat of counter-force nuclear retaliation in which every effort is made to avoid damage to large population centers not be enough to deter nuclear aggression by a power willing to attack cities? The devastation of counter-force warfare would be an extraordinarily high price to pay for the war aims of the aggressor. On the other hand, an aggressor willing to risk such losses might not be amenable to the pressures of graduated retaliation leading to selective counter-city warfare by the victim of his attack.

This discussion is only meaningful in terms of just war theory if the rigid principle of non-combatant immunity from intentional, direct attack is rejected (or the escape hatch of double effect herein rejected, is left open). In the extensive counter-force strikes which we have been discussing, there is the certainty that many non-combatants will inevitably die. They will be far fewer than in the case of counter-city warfare but the number will still be large. In terms of the principle of proportionality, that number might not be disproportionate to the good ends of deterring further attacks by a nuclear aggressor and reducing the capability to launch such attacks.

With the increasing hardening and dispersion of the means of delivering nuclear weapons, counter-force war will become much more difficult. The difficulties will further increase as active defense means are developed. The result will be that the number and destructive power of nuclear weapons required in counter-force strikes will be so great that they will inflict ever greater damage on the target society. Thus we must honestly face the fact that by retaliating "only" with counter-force nuclear means we are still engaging in a horrendous act of war. Such an act must surely be justified only by the desperate necessity to prevent the destruction of one's own society.

Once the necessity of nuclear retaliation to defend one's society ceased, the right to use such means would cease. If the enemy attacks ceased, there should be immediate cessation of one's own attacks. If the enemy's attacks continued to the point where one's own society was so damaged that no reasonable purpose could be served by continuing the war, retaliatory strikes should cease. Continuation of the war for vengeance would be an understandable human act but its gross immorality should be manifest.

One alternative solution to the dilemmas of nuclear deterrence has been suggested. It is argued that since the whole point of establishing deterrents is to insure insofar as possible that they will never have to be used, it is legitimate to mount a deterrent force and strike a posture that threatens damage that would not only be unacceptable to an aggressor but immoral. But, it is argued, the party maintaining such a deterrent could privately have a firm resolution never to use the deterrent force to its fullest, immoral extent. Thus one obtains the advantages of a terrifying and highly effective deterrent threat without having to execute it. Alternatively, it has been argued that the mere possession of means that could destroy an aggressor's whole society is a sufficient deterrent in itself, even if the possessor of such means openly admits that he would not use them beyond a point set by his moral standards. No responsible enemy decision-maker, it is argued, could afford to take a chance on the victim's adhesion to limits based on moral scruples once a war was under way.

There is much to be said for this argument. It finds some support in the existing ambiguity of Western policy on first use of nuclear weapons against a conventional attack and uncertainty as to the form that graduated deterrence might take. But one is reluctant to complicate the already complex psychological-sociological-political aspects of deterrence by introducing explicit or implied threats that are not intended to be executed. The requirements of such a deterrent strategy in terms of moral commitment and restraint appear to be prohibitive. The conclusion of this writer is that one should threaten only what he will do and has a moral right to do in the event of aggression.

In summary, it is believed that the United States would meet the standards that are emerging from papal and conciliar treatment of the problems of nuclear war and deterrence by following these policies:

(1) No first recourse to armed force of any kind except as enforcement action validly authorized by the UN or other international organizations.

(2) No first use of nuclear weapons.

(3) No counter-city warfare, *i.e.*, the execution of an attack in which a city as such is the target or in which the military target is so situated that destruction of all or a major part of a whole city is inevitable.

(4) Counter-force retaliation for aggressor's first use of nuclear weapons which is proportionate to the requirements of deterring further attacks and reducing the aggressor's capability to continue them until the attacks cease or resistance ceases to be reasonable.

(5) Nuclear powers should explore every possibility of diminishing their dependence upon the threat of nuclear deterrents through progress in arms control and disarmament and they should prevent the spread of nuclear weapons through effective nonproliferation agreements and policies.

How practical are these recommended policies? The first has been U.S. policy throughout this century. There are no clear-cut major cases of the U.S. violating this prescription. There is, of course, disagreement over the facts in cases such as the military intervention in Vietnam, but the American justification of resort to armed coercion is based on the invitation of an indigenous government and on the right of collective self-defense against either direct or indirect aggression. We all know the different opinions on the facts in this case, but it is clear that the United States does not assert the right to initiate an offensive war of aggression.

Of course, not all Americans accept the renunciation of first use of armed coercion, *e.g.*, advocates of an invasion of Castro's Cuba and of preventive attacks on Red China. These Americans should be told that their position is contrary to international law which, through the UN Charter and many other treaties, is also the law of the land. It is also contrary to the teaching of the Church concerning respect for international law in general and on the obligation to avoid recourse to armed force except in cases of self-defense in particular. To repeat, aggressive first-use of armed coercion by the United States would violate the pledges of every modern American President.

The second recommended policy, no first-use of nuclear weapons, admittedly raises some difficult questions. First, there is the problem of defining "first-use." If there were certainty that an enemy nuclear attack was about to be launched, would a pre-emptive first strike constitute first-use? Presumably, a moralist would hesitate to answer this question in the abstract. He would want the facts of a concrete case.

Secondly, a no first-use rule might in practice be difficult to reconcile with the fifth recommendation against the proliferation of nuclear weapons. Most proposals for non-proliferation are accompanied by suggestions that the nuclear powers guarantee the security of the non-nuclear states who renounce the acquisition of nuclear weapons. Suppose, for example, the United States promises to protect India from nuclear blackmail by a state such as Communist China. Should the U.S. be required to tell the Indians that it will only retaliate with nuclear weapons after an aggressive first-strike has actually taken place in India? This is a problem that will require considerable discussion as we press our efforts to prevent proliferation. Clear adhesion to a no first-use of nuclears policy would also seriously affect the areas such as Western Europe where calculated ambiguity is part of the deterrent. Whether the U.S. Government will agree to abandon this ambiguity remains to be seen.

The third and fourth suggested policies are open to many criticisms. On the one hand it can be questioned whether the counter-city - counter-force distinction would be meaningful in the event of extensive counter-force nuclear attacks, particularly if they caused heavy fall-out. About all that can be said is that every effort should be made to reduce as much as possible the damage done to population centers. The success of such efforts will be determined to a considerable extent by geography, by the disposition of the enemy's forces and installations, and by the character of the decision-makers on both sides. The governments can make it more or less difficult for the enemy to avoid strikes which will directly destroy their populations. The moral fiber of the leaders will be sorely tested if their own population centers are hit directly and retaliation in kind is demanded. But the moral imperatives laid down by modern popes and Vatican Council II clearly require that every possible effort be made to minimize the effects of belligerent actions on enemy populations.

With Herman Kahn and Secretary McNamara, the author feels that there are degrees of the "unthinkable". Counter-force warfare and graduated deterrence may require threatening and doing "unthinkable" things but massive retaliation with counter-city warfare as the immediate reaction to a nuclear (or even conventional) aggression is more unthinkable and clearly more reprehensible from a moral standpoint.

There remains a further point to be made about counter-city warfare. It is a controverted point which is under discussion in the United States as these words are written and may have been resolved in one way or another by the time this book appears. This concerns extensive counter-city attacks with conventional air raids. At the moment, there is a debate about bombing Hanoi. It should be clear that insofar as Catholic teaching is concerned, a conventional "obliteration" or "city-busting" raid of the World War II variety with the purpose of substantially destroying a whole city and breaking the enemy's will to resist is immoral. Antecedent counter-city attacks would raise the difficult questions of retaliation in kind discussed here in terms of nuclear retaliation. But there is no imminent danger of large-scale air attacks on Saigon and other South Vietnamese cities. It should be clear that, in Catholic teaching, conventional counter-city attacks in the context of a war like that in Vietnam are not morally permissible.

By "counter-city" attacks I mean attacks on an entire city as such, *e.g.,* the attacks on British and German cities in World War II. The attacks on oil depots near or even in Hanoi or Haiphong are not counter-city attacks. As executed by the United States, they have been attacks against legitimate military targets and they have been proportionate to reasonable military goals. Likewise, air attacks in South Vietnam which frequently kill civilians and destroy their property are not counter-city or counter-people attacks. Individual attacks may be condemned because of their indiscriminate nature arising out of miscalculation, incorrect information, accident, or wrong intention on the part of those responsible for them. But they cannot be condemned *en bloc* simply because non-combatants in substantial numbers are killed by them. All armed conflict in a populated area involves the death of non-combatants. What is not permitted is "any act of war aimed indiscriminately at the destruction of entire cities or of extensive areas along with their population."

The fifth recommendation is in consonance with official U.S. policy. However, the definition of "progress" and the assessment of priorities and risks in U.S. foreign and defense policies as they affect such "progress" is a highly controversial subject. One has but to read books such as Bernhard C. Bechhoefer's *Postwar Negotiations for Arms Control* or Harold Karen Jacobson and Eric Stein's *Diplomats, Scientists, and Politicians* to learn how variable is the will for progress in arms control and disarmament in the U.S. Government and in American society.

In summary, the policies here proposed generally coincide with the main lines of U.S. policy but on important points they go beyond it in limiting the threat or use of nuclear weapons. It should be noted that these proposals go *far* beyond the limitations that would be acceptable to many of those who supported Senator Goldwater's positions on this subject in 1964 and who today urge policies in Asia based on massive and generally indiscriminate use of air power, possibly including nuclear weapons.

Since this book is directed particularly to Americans, we shall only mention in passing the implications of our discussions for lesser nuclear powers, such as France, which aspire to a deterrent based (for the foreseeable future) solely on counter-city warfare. It is to be hoped that Christians and men of good will in those countries are pondering the implications of modern Catholic thought on war and peace for their nation's future policies.

8
Arms Control and Disarmament

The preceding chapters should have made clear the practical and moral desirability of arms control and disarmament. This chapter is not intended to be a comprehensive treatment of the subjects. What is intended here is to indicate the interrelationships between defense theory and policy and arms control. Our problem is not so much the eliminating of armed force as of reducing and restricting it in such a way as to insure that the remaining force will be preponderately channeled toward the maintenance of international law and order and not toward the goals of selfish power politics.

We can distinguish three approaches to arms control and disarmament, which overlap somewhat, as do the terms themselves. Arms control generally means reducing the most dangerous and provocative weapons and situations, measures to maintain the "balance" between sides in an arms race, and some arms reduction. The emphasis is more on balance, stability and continued security for the parties, than on reduction. Disarmament means mainly reduction in armaments, although many disarmament suggestions include features similar to the arms control approach. Today, as in the name of the U.S. agency primarily concerned with these problems, The Arms Control and Disarmament Agency, it is increasingly the practice to link the two terms. The three main approaches seem to be:

(1) *Unilateral Disarmament.* It is argued that if one side were to take substantial steps toward disarmament, the other would follow. Alternately, some argue that there is a moral obligation to start disarming, regardless of reciprocation by the other side. The

success of the voluntary test-ban of some years ago encouraged this approach. Its breach by the Soviets reduced optimism on this kind of policy. It is not generally taken too seriously in official Western nor Communist circles and has not been advocated by the hierarchy of the Church or by most moralists and authorities on the subject.

(2) *Arms Control and Disarmament Based on Trust.* There are several forms of this approach. It may be unfair to list them together but they all emphasize the role of mutual trust in arms control and disarmament:

(a) Treaties without sanctions except through international tribunals and the influence of world opinion. Some urge that we draw up a comprehensive treaty on the subject and trust in the willingness of the parties to abide by their international agreements. If they do not, the remedies of the International Court of Justice, the U.N. system, etc., as well as world public opinion, are said to be sufficient sanctions. The Geneva Protocol of 1925 outlawing gas and bacteriological warfare is given as a precedent. However, the Geneva Protocol has been observed for many extra-legal reasons, not the least of which is the fact that all of the major powers have BC deterrents, *i.e.,* the means to retaliate in kind. Neither the general experience of the international law of war nor the record of Communist respect for treaties resting solely on faith and international law encourages support for this approach. However, it must be pointed out that such treaties often seem attractive to people who know little of international law and politics and who mistakenly believe that we can "legislate" for our conflict-torn international society as we do for the United States.

(b) Plans for comprehensive arms control and disarmament by stages. This approach, developed by leading experts on the subject, seems to be the basic U.S. approach. The idea is to list a number of objectives which total up to GCD, General and Complete Disarmament, wherein only internal security forces and some kind of international peace force will exist. To reach GCD from the balance of terror, we must proceed by stages from comparatively modest mutual concessions (like the 1963 ban on testing in the air and on the sea) to agreements requiring a considerable degree of mutual faith. The very experience of hammering out agreements and the establishment of expectations that they will be kept, might well lead to increasing mutual trust. However, some degree of inspection and verification will accompany some of the measures.

This approach combines a certain amount of trust and reliance on purely legal commitments with provisions to check up on compliance through inspections. Because it is worked out in phases, it has a built-in sanction or the possibility for self-help. At any point where the agreements are seriously violated the other parties can restore the previous situation, or at least regain their independence of action. The risks of losing out to a violator are much smaller than in the so-called "paper ban" but there are still risks of a comparative loss of strength as a result of cheating or major violations by the other side.

(3) *The Controlled Balance of Power.* This third approach blends into the comprehensive arms control and disarmament concept. Perhaps the difference is more of emphasis, attitude, willingness to make explicit the power basis for a successful arms control *régime*. It begins with the assumption that the key to disarmament is security. No responsible government is going to jeopardize its security to make progress toward disarmament. So, it is argued, we should bring this fact into the open, and indeed, build on it. At each point in arms control and disarmament negotiations, there should be an objective analysis of the balance of power and how it would probably be affected by the proposed reductions, changes or restraints. Every effort must be made to insure that such changes will be fair to both sides. In this way real progress will be possible, with emphasis not on precarious inspections, unenforced law, or mutual faith, but on a system of checks and balances not unlike the classical balance of power in 18th and 19th century international politics. With security assured and the balance always protected, states will have a practical interest in participating in comparatively "safe" arms control measures to reduce the self-defeating arms race and nuclear brinksmanship which all agree is in no one's "national interest."

If, in the course of such balanced arms control developments a certain amount of mutual trust and understanding and some new international law were to develop, so much the better. But this approach begins with practical power politics and works toward more idealistic results rather than aspiring to an early outbreak of international idealism. A full critique of this approach is not possible here. If it sounds safer and more attractive to some, we should point out that insuring a "stable balance" indefinitely is a very complex and difficult task, particularly in a time of changes brought about artificially by arms control.

This approach is not divorced, however, from the comprehensive arms control and disarmament-by-stages approach. The latter, after all, assumes the nuclear balance of terror. It does not always emphasize it; rather it may play it down depending on the "audience". But the balance of power approach, while willing to explore many of the specific parts of the comprehensive arms control scheme, always insists that this kind of thing should only proceed under the "umbrella of nuclear deterrence."

Some Moral Implications of the Three Approaches

How do these approaches stand up under moral scrutiny?

(1) Disarmament by treaty would offer no difficulties to the moralist, or would it? Is it responsible, is it moral, to leave one's nation (and others dependent on it) bereft of effective means of defense? We have here a problem that was paramount in the 1930's when well-meaning people insisted on disarmament and unilateral dismantling of defenses at a time when force was badly needed to protect freedom and justice against totalitarian oppressors. On the record, major unverified disarmament solely on the basis of a paper ban based on faith and respect for international law would appear to be irresponsible. The Church has not asked Western statesmen to risk so much on faith in the enemy.

(2) The comprehensive arms control and disarmament-by-stages approach seems close to the ideas in *Pacem in Terris,* the *Pastoral Constitution on the Church in the Modern World,* and other official pronouncements of the Church. Its positive features seem to elicit active support from the Church. However, there is the problem of the "umbrella of nuclear deterrence." Although

this is soft pedaled, it remains the basis for contemporary arms control agreements. If one side, through moral scruples, decided that what it was threatening and preparing to do was immoral and ought to be stopped, are we not back to unilateral disarmament? The other side would have little reason to "negotiate" disarmament with a nation already in the process of unilateral disarmament. No matter how enlightened our comprehensive arms control and disarmament "package" may look, it depends for years to come on the continuation of some kind of deterrent posture on both sides.

(3) The foregoing aspect of our problem is clear when we look at it in terms of the "balance of power" approach. There is an explicit element here that is only implicit in the comprehensive plan-by-stages schemes, namely the manipulation of nuclear power to preserve order. So the balance of power approach requires moral acceptance or rejection of the position that it is legitimate to threaten the things needed to maintain a "stable" balance of terror as an "umbrella" to cover the progressive negotiation of arms control and disarmament agreements.

This approach also collides with the whole "idealistic" notion of the role of power in politics, whether domestic or international, that permeates much of Catholic thought, particularly *Pacem in Terris*. The modern advocates of balance of power tend to believe, along with Alexander Hamilton and other "realists," that some kind of "power politics" is normal in societies of all kinds. They believe that the job of political, legal, and moral theory is not to try to eliminate power but to institutionalize its uses so as to negate anti-social forces and maximize the power of the community. Schemes such as those of Professor Sohn and, indeed, the official U.S. disarmament plan, look for a day when we come to the "end" of war, power politics, and the like and live under the "rule of law." The realists foresee a perpetual need for power politics, hence for power balances and guidelines, as long as men are men and not angels.

Catholic authorities are to be found on both sides of the "idealist-realist" debate. I would contend that *actually* the natural law tradition is closer to the realists in that it accepts the phenomenon of power and seeks to regulate it. On the other hand, papal statements, particularly in our time, have been quite idealistic. *Pacem in Terris* seems to have tipped the balance toward the idealism of the "rule of law" under general and complete disarmament concepts. Still the Church is at pains to reiterate that it has not forgotten the injustices that continue to be visited upon hundreds of millions of human beings. Recent authoritative Catholic sources can be cited in support of the realist view. Pope Paul's Message to the U.N. and the *Pastoral Constitution on the Church in the Modern World* both condition hopes for peace based on mutual trust, on the improvement of sinful man whose failings may threaten conflict until the end of the world.

The foregoing analysis may be a bit abrupt and unfair to arms control and disarmament specialists as well as to the Church officials and moralists who deal with contemporary problems of war and peace. We have been trying to bring together and analyze the main concepts, policies and factors in our problem. When we allude to the position of this or that individual or organization or school of thought, we must introduce it into our own analytical framework. This can sometimes be misleading. But it is necessary if we are to come to a fundamental analysis of our problems of morality, defense policy and arms control and disarmament. At the risk, therefore, of some over-simplification, let us look at the present situation in the following way:

The mainstream of arms control and disarmament efforts goes in the direction of stage-by-stage comprehensive arms control under a gradually diminishing umbrella of nuclear deterrence. Despite differences in emphasis within this mainstream, the foundation of all of these efforts is the balance of terror, with small, gradually increasing elements of mutual trust and shared objectives introduced wherever possible. This is the "great consensus" among experts in America. In *other* Western countries of any military importance (except perhaps Britain) the emphasis upon deterrence and the deprecation of mutual trust becomes noticeably greater, *e.g.,* in France and Germany. This is the central fact of our efforts to alter the balance of terror. Ironically, such efforts begin by building on the balance of terror.

We have seen that the recent teaching of the Church has left a little more room and a little more time for the process of working out the details of morally permissible nuclear deterrence during the first stages of a process wherein arms control and disarmament and the strengthening of international law and organization go forward. Obviously, the longer this process takes, the greater the dangers both of physical destruction and immoral behavior. In whatever remaining "interlude" we have, the following tasks should be accomplished:

(1) The moral issues regarding the mounting and use of nuclear deterrent systems must be further clarified. This calls for intensive study by moralists and experts in the relevant technical disciplines to determine as specifically as possible what is being done, what morally can be done, and what hope exists for narrowing any gap between the two. The most important issues would appear to be: clarification of the status of the principle of non-combatant immunity from intentional direct attack and of interpretations thereof based on the principle of double effect, the possibility that there is moral support for a no-first-use rule for nuclear war, and the permissibility of retaliatory counter-force war which while neither "total" nor "out of control" inevitably produces grave damage.

(2) In the light of the findings with respect to the first set of issues, moralists and experts in appropriate disciplines should seek to determine what concrete measures for arms control and disarmament and the strengthening of international law and organization are necessary and feasible in a pluralistic world.

The Church now needs to set intermediate goals. We know that we must move from the terrible trap of arms race and the balance of terror. We have a vague vision of a disarmed world governed by a world authority. As we assess our progress toward these goals, we need more explicit intermediate goals and time-tables. One of the greatest deficiencies in existing Catholic teaching is its propensity for mixing immediate goals, such as finding a solution to wars in progress or taking immediate action to help the world's starving millions, and long-range goals, such as the establishment of world authority acceptable to Christians, Communists, and the heterogeneous "Third World." This last will not take place very soon, but how soon is "soon" and how much progress is satisfactory?

As the *Pastoral Constitution on the Church in the Modern*

World emphasized, these tasks are, *inter alia,* the proper responsibility of institutions of higher learning, research institutes, associations in support of international peace, law and order, and of all institutions and individuals who have the ability to contribute to their successful accomplishment.

Questions for Catholics

M any subjects could be suggested for scrutiny and discussion. Some of them should occupy the thoughts of the concerned Catholic:

(1) How do you rate the efforts of your government to avoid nuclear war without surrendering and, at the same time, to begin the road to arms control and disarmament?

(a) Do you believe that the energies, budget allotments, talent, time, etc., of the Administration devoted to arms control and disarmament are enough? (How much information do you have about all this?)

(b) How does the Congress in general and your Senators and Representatives in particular rate in terms of demonstrated efforts to help this country develop defense-arms control policies that most closely accord with Christian principles?

(c) At all levels of government, how honest and sincere are the efforts for realistic arms control and disarmament measures? How do words compare with deeds and how do words vary according to the audience?

(d) Have you ever read the United States and Soviet proposals for General and Complete Disarmament? What do you think of them?

(e) What is your opinion on the Draft Treaty to Prevent the Spread of Nuclear Weapons tabled by the U.S. at the August 17, 1965 plenary meeting in Geneva of the Eighteen-Nation Disarmament Conference?

(f) What about United States disarmament negotiations? Have we been consistent, fair, honest, technically prepared, in our arms control negotiations?

(g) Are you convinced that our Armed Forces consistently try to find practical alternatives to forms of warfare that are questionable from the moral point of view?

(2) Is the Church playing its proper role in the world and in the United States?

(a) How do you rate the extent to which pronouncements on questions of war and deterrence by the popes, the hierarchy, respected Catholic moralists, scholars, lay leaders, and the Catholic press, are informed, relevant, and responsive to the moral dilemmas we face?

(b) How would you rate the performance of our schools, our faculties, our students, and our research organizations on these points?

(3) Where do you stand in all of this? What will be the "state of the question" in another twenty years? What are your responsibilities of contributing to and understanding a "great debate" which has already been over twenty years in getting underway?

Appendix A

DRAFT SCHEMA 13 — 1964

(Reprinted from *Peace, The Churches, and the Bomb,* James Finn, ed., published by the Council on Religion and International Affairs, 1965.)

A mong the principal signs of the times there stands out clearly before all men an immense desire for true and lasting peace, although the human race after so many bloody wars is still disturbed by almost continuous conflicts, and is terrified by new weapons capable of destroying the entire family. In view of this extreme danger the barbarity of war stands out in an entirely new light. For this reason, the Church, the handmaiden of the peace of Christ, has to work with the greatest diligence, together with the entire family of nations which is the family of God. And she wills that peace, which transcends every desire and work of this world, may bear fruit among all people. This Sacred Council, replying to the suppliant voices reaching her from all sides, before God adjures all men, all nations, and particularly the rulers of nations, to be mindful of their very grave responsibility, and in view of the complexity of the situation to work with united forces for the establishment of peace:

1. Peace is made stable and lasting by mutual friendship and mutual help, effectively recognizing the united will to help, or "solidarity," which ought to govern the family of nations. There is no true peace, if wars are only postponed by a parity of weapons for spreading terror, rather than a sincere spirit of cooperation and concord. Therefore, everything that unfortunately divides rather than unites must be adjudged as opposed to peace, and above all any words, doctrines or actions that spread hatred, contempt, vengeance, or unfounded suspicion against any nation or

even stir up an excessive patriotism and that burning desire to acquire excessive power. Everyone, therefore, and especially those who exert any influence on public opinion, must speak the things that are of peace, promoting mutual esteem among the nations, gladly extolling the virtues of other nations, speaking only patiently and calmly of their defects, and promoting mutual respect among different persuasions.

2. The controversies that may perchance arise between nations must not be settled by force and arms, but by treaties and agreements. Although, after all the aids of peaceful discussion have been exhausted, it may not be illicit, when one's rights have been unjustly hampered, to defend those rights against such unjust aggression by violence and force, nevertheless the use of arms, especially nuclear weapons, whose effects are greater than can be imagined and therefore cannot be reasonably regulated by men, exceeds all just proportion and therefore must be judged before God and man as most wicked. Every honest effort therefore must be made, so that not only nuclear warfare may be solemnly proscribed by all nations and alliances as an enormous crime, but also that nuclear arms or others of like destructive force may be utterly destroyed and banned.

3. Since the terrifying destructive force, which is daily increasing in war arms, is able to cause calamities and horrible destruction throughout the world, and since technological progress, communications and organizations for peacefully settling disputes are daily proving more effective, it is becoming ever more absurd that war is an instrument suited for the redressing of violated rights.

Therefore the Sacred Council denounces as a ruinous injury inflicted upon the whole human family, and in severest terms censures, the uncontrollable armaments race, inasmuch as it is injurious to and prevents real peace, harmony and trust among nations, places a great part of mankind in danger of their lives, and dissipates the wealth needed for much better things.

The rulers of state should be thoroughly aware of the fact that it is their duty to deliver their people from this danger by agreements which will effectively work out a just peace and at the same time they must endeavor to put out of men's minds all hostility, hatred and mistrust. Better aids must be chosen to prevent wars and peacefully remove conflicts; among these aids are the following: consistent progress in building up a universal community among the nations, all of which will remain free; an international authority having at its disposal the means necessary to avoid war and to promote peace, so as to bring about conditions in which war of any kind can no longer be regarded as a legitimate instrument, even for the defense of one's own rights.

4. Let the faithful who believe in Christ the Lord, the Prince of Peace, feel his impelling love and in all gladness follow him, who by the blood of his cross reconciled all men to God and restored the unity of all in the one family of God, and in his own flesh killed hatred. Let the faithful therefore shun no sacrifice, so that, practising the truth in love (cf. Eph. 4, 15), they may in every way contribute toward establishing a lasting peace, which is a sign of the world redeemed. Let them, by their charity, justice and unity, be harbingers of the peace of Christ.

Appendix B

THE PASTORAL CONSTITUTION ON THE CHURCH IN THE MODERN WORLD

CHAPTER FIVE
MAINTENANCE OF PEACE AND ESTABLISHMENT OF A COMMUNITY OF NATIONS

Introduction

77. In our generation which has been marked by the persistent and acute hardships and anxiety resulting from the ravages of war and the threat of war, the whole human race faces a moment of supreme crisis in its advance toward maturity. Mankind has gradually come closer together and is everywhere more conscious of its own unity; but it will not succceed in accomplish-

ing the task awaiting it, that is, the establishment of a truly human world for all men over the entire earth, unless everyone devotes himself to the cause of true peace with renewed vigor. Thus the message of the Gospel, which epitomizes the highest ideals and aspirations of mankind, shines anew in our times when it proclaims that the advocates of peace are blessed "for they shall be called sons of God" (Mt. 5, 9).

Accordingly, the Council proposes to outline the true and noble nature of peace, to condemn the savagery of war, and earnestly to exhort Christians to cooperate with all in securing a peace based on justice and charity and in promoting the means necessary to attain it, under the help of Christ, author of peace.

Nature of Peace

78. Peace is more than the absence of war: it cannot be reduced to the maintenance of a balance of power between opposing forces nor does it arise out of despotic dominion, but it is appropriately called "the effect of righteousness" (Is. 32, 17). It is the fruit of that right ordering of things, with which the divine Founder has invested human society and which must be actualized by man thirsting after an ever more perfect reign of justice. But while the common good of mankind ultimately derives from the eternal law, it depends in the concrete upon circumstances which change as time goes on; consequently, peace will never be achieved once and for all but must be built up continually. Since, moreover, human nature is weak and wounded by sin, the achievement of peace requires a constant effort to control the passions and unceasing vigilance by lawful authority.

But this is not enough. Peace cannot be obtained on earth unless the welfare of man is safeguarded and people freely and trustingly share with one another the riches of their minds and their talents. A firm determination to respect the dignity of other men and other peoples along with the deliberate practice of fraternal love are absolutely necessary for the achievement of peace. Accordingly, peace is also the fruit of love, for love goes beyond what justice can ensure.

Peace on earth, which flows from love of one's neighbor, symbolizes and derives from the peace of Christ who proceeds from God the Father. Christ, the Word made flesh, the Prince of peace, reconciled all men to God by the cross, and, restoring the unity of all in one people and one body, he abolished hatred in his own flesh; after being lifted up through his resurrection he poured forth the Spirit of love into the hearts of men. Therefore, all Christians are earnestly to speak the truth in love (cf. Eph. 4, 15) and join with all peace-loving men in pleading for peace and trying to bring it about. In the same spirit we cannot but express our admiration for all who forgo the use of violence to vindicate their rights and resort to those means of defense which are also available to weaker parties, provided it can be done without hardship to the rights and duties of others and of the community.

Insofar as men are sinners, the threat of war hangs over them and will so continue until the coming of Christ; but insofar as they can vanquish sin by coming together in charity, violence itself will be vanquished and they will make these words come true: "They shall beat their swords into ploughshares, and their spears into pruning hooks; nation shall not lift up sword against nation, neither shall they learn war any more" (Is. 2, 4).

SECTION 1: AVOIDANCE OF WAR

Curbing the Savagery of War

79. Even though recent wars have wrought immense material and moral havoc on the world, the devastation of battle still rages in some part of the world. Indeed, now that every kind of weapon produced by modern science is used in war, the savagery of war threatens to lead the combatants to barbarities far surpassing those of former ages. Moreover, the complexity of the modern world and the intricacy of international relations cause wars that have lain dormant to be protracted by new methods of

infiltration and subversion. In many cases terrorist methods are regarded as new strategies of war.

Faced by this deplorable state of humanity the Council wishes to remind men that the natural law of peoples and its universal principles still retain their binding force. The conscience of mankind firmly and ever more emphatically proclaims these principles. Any action which deliberately violates these principles and any order which commands such actions is criminal and blind obedience cannot excuse those who carry them out. The most infamous among these actions are those designed for the reasoned and methodical extermination of an entire race, nation, or ethnic minority. These must be condemned as frightful crimes; and we cannot commend too highly the courage of the men who openly and fearlessly resist those who issue orders of this kind.

On the question of warfare, there are various international conventions, signed by many countries, aimed at rendering military action and its consequences less inhuman; they deal with the treatment of wounded and interned prisoners of war and with various kindred questions. These agreements must be preserved; indeed public authorities and specialists in these matters must do all in their power to improve these conventions and thus bring about a better and more effective curbing of the savagery of war. Moreover, it seems just that humane laws should regulate the case of conscientious objectors who refuse to carry arms, provided some other form of community service is substituted.

War, of course, has not ceased to be part of the human scene. As long as the danger of war persists and there is no international authority with the necesssary competence and power, governments cannot be denied the right of lawful self-defense, once all peace efforts have failed. State leaders and all who share the burdens of public administration have the duty to defend the interests of their people and to conduct such grave matters with a deep sense of responsibility. However, it is one thing to wage a war of self-defense; it is quite another to seek to impose domination on another nation. The possession of war potential does not justify the use of force for political or military objectives. Nor does the mere fact that war has unfortunately broken out mean that all is fair between the warring parties.

All those who enter the military service in loyalty to their country should look upon themselves as the custodians of the security and freedom of their fellow-countrymen; and when they carry out their duty properly, they are contributing to the maintenance of peace.

Total Warfare

80. The development of armaments by modern science has immeasurably magnified the horrors and wickedness of war. Warfare conducted with these weapons can inflict immense and indiscriminate havoc which goes far beyond the bounds of legitimate defense. Indeed if the kind of weapons now stocked in the arsenals of the great powers were to be employed to the fullest, the result would only be the almost complete reciprocal slaughter of one side by the other, not to speak of the widespread devastation that would follow in the world and the deadly after-effects resulting from the use of such arms.

All these factors force us to undertake a completely fresh reappraisal of war. Men of this generation should realize that they will have to render an account of their warlike behavior; the destiny of generations to come depends largely on the decisions they make today.

With these considerations in mind the Council, endorsing the condemnations of total warfare issued by recent popes, declares: Every act of war directed to the indiscriminate destruction of whole cities or vast areas with their inhabitants is a crime against God and man, which merits firm and unequivocal condemnation.

The hazards peculiar to modern warfare consist in the fact that they expose those possessing recently developed weapons to the risk of perpetrating crimes like these and, by an inexorable chain of events, of urging men to even worse acts of atrocity. To obviate the possibility of this happening at any time in the future, the bishops of the world gathered together implore all men, especially government leaders and military advisors, to give unceasing consideration to their immense responsibilities before God and before the whole human race.

The Arms Race

81. Undoubtedly, armaments are not amassed merely for use in wartime. Since the defensive strength of any nation is thought to depend on its capacity of immediate retaliation, the stockpiling of arms which grows from year to year, serves, in a way hitherto unthought of, as a deterrent to potential attackers. Many people look upon this as the most effective way known at the present time for maintaining some sort of peace among nations.

Whatever one may think of this form of deterrent, people are convinced that the arms race, which quite a few countries have entered, is no infallible way for maintaining real peace and that the resulting so-called balance of power is no sure and genuine path to achieving it. Rather than eliminate the causes of war, the arms race serves only to aggravate the position. As long as extravagant sums of money are poured into the development of new weapons, it is impossible to devote adequate aid to tackling the misery which prevails at the present day in the world. Instead of eradicating international conflict once and for all, the contagion is spreading to other parts of the world. New approaches, based on a renewal of mentality, will have to be chosen in order to remove this stumbling-block, to free the earth from its pressing anxieties, and give back to the world a genuine peace.

Therefore, we declare once again: the arms race is one of the greatest curses on the human race and the harm it inflicts on the poor is more than can be endured. And there is every reason to fear that if it continues it will bring forth those lethal disasters which are already in preparation. Warned by the possibility of the catastrophes that man has created let us profit by the respite we now enjoy, thanks to divine favor, to take stock of our responsibilities and find ways of resolving controversies in a manner more worthy of human beings. Providence urgently demands of us that we free ourselves from the age-old slavery of war. If we refuse to make this effort, there is no knowing where we will be led on the fatal path we have taken.

Total Outlawing of War: International Action To Prevent War

82. It is our clear duty to spare no effort in order to work for the moment when all war will be completely outlawed by international agreement. This goal, of course, requires the establishment of a universally acknowledged public authority vested with the effective power to ensure security for all, regard for justice, and respect for law. But before this desirable authority can be constituted, it is necessary for existing international bodies to devote themselves resolutely to the exploration of better means for obtaining common security. But since peace must be born of mutual trust between peoples instead of being forced on nations through dread of arms, all must work to put an end to the arms race and make a real beginning of disarmament, not unilaterally indeed but at an equal rate on all sides, on the basis of agreements and backed up by genuine and effective guarantees.

In the meantime one must not underestimate the efforts already made or now under way to eliminate the danger of war. On the contrary, support should be given to the good will of numerous individuals who are making every effort to eliminate the havoc of war; these men, although burdened by the weighty responsibilities of their high office, are motivated by a consciousness of their very grave obligations, even if they cannot ignore the complexity of the situation as it stands. We must beseech the Lord to give them the strength to tackle with perseverance and carry out with courage this task of supreme love for man which is the building up of a lasting peace in a true spirit of manhood. In our times this work demands that they enlarge their thoughts and their spirit beyond the confines of their own country, that they put aside nationalistic selfishness and ambitions to dominate other nations, and that they cultivate deep reverence for the whole of mankind which is painstakingly advancing toward greater maturity.

The problems of peace and disarmament have been treated at length with courage and untiring consultation at negotiations and international meetings; these are to be considered as the first steps toward the solutions of such important questions and must be further pursued with even greater insistence, with a view to obtaining concrete results in the future. But people should beware of leaving these problems to the efforts of a few men without putting their own attitudes in order. For state leaders, who are at once the guardians of their own people and the promotors of the welfare of the whole world, rely to a large extent on public opinion and public attitudes. Their peace-making efforts will be in vain, as long as men are divided and warring among themselves through hostility, contempt, and distrust, as well as through racial hatred and uncompromising hostilities. Hence there is a very urgent need of re-education and renewed orientation of public opinion. Those engaged in the work of education, especially youth education, and the people who mold public opinion, should regard it as their most important task to educate the minds of men to renewed sentiments of peace. Every one of us needs a change of heart; we must set our gaze on the whole world and look to those tasks we can all perform together in order to bring about the betterment of our race.

But let us not be buoyed up with false hope. For unless animosity and hatred are put aside, and firm, honest agreements about world peace are concluded, humanity may, in spite of the wonders of modern science, go from the grave crisis of the present day to that dismal hour, when the only peace it will experience will be the dread peace of death. The Church, however, living in the midst of these anxieties, even as it makes these statements, has not lost hope. The Church intends to propose to our age over and over again, in season and out of season, the Apostle's message: "Behold, now is the acceptable time" for a change of heart, "behold, now is the day of salvation."

Bibliography

JUST WAR THEORY: MORALITY AND NUCLEAR WAR

A. Books

Allers, Ulrich S. and O'Brien, William V., *Christian Ethics and Nuclear Warfare*. Washington, Institute of World Polity, Georgetown University, 1963.
Atomare Kampf Mittel und Christliche Ethik. Diskussions Beiträge Deutscher Katholiken. Munich, Kösel-Verlag K.G., 1960.
Bennett, John C. (ed.), *Nuclear Weapons and the Conflict of Conscience*. New York, Scribner's, 1962.
Bosc, Robert, *La société internationale et l'Eglise*. Paris, Editions SPES, 1961, especially "Premiere partie: Les Tensions Internationales," Ch. I-VII, pp. 11-244.
Brière, Yves de la, *Le droit de juste guerre*. Paris, Pedone, 1933.
Clancy, William (ed.), *The Moral Dilemma of Nuclear Weapons, Essays from Worldview*. New York, The Council on Religion and International Affairs, 1961.
Coste, René, *Le Problème du droit de guerre dans la pensée de Pie XII*. Paris, Aubier, 1961.
Eppstein, John, *The Catholic Tradition of the Law of Nations*. Washington, Carnegie Endowment for International Peace; and the Catholic Association for International Peace, 1935.
——— (trans., ed., and commentator). *Code of International Ethics*. Westminster, Maryland, Newman Press, 1953.
Falk, Richard A., *Law, Morality and War in the Contemporary World*. Princeton, Princeton University Press, 1963.
Finn, James (ed.), *Peace, the Churches, and the Bomb*. New York, The Council on Religion and International Affairs, 1965.
Fleischmann, Rudolf, *Kann der atomare Verteidigungskrieg ein gerechter Krieg sein?* Munich, K. Zink Verlag, 1960.
Hörman, Karl, *Peace and Modern War in the Judgment of the Church*, trans. by Sister Mary Caroline Hemesath, O.S.F. Westminster, Md., Newman Press, 1966.

111

Jaspers, Karl, *The Future of Mankind*. Chicago, University of Chicago Press, 1958.

McReavy, L.L., *Peace and War in Catholic Doctrine*. Oxford, Catholic Social Guild, 1963.

Messner, Johannes, *Social Ethics,* trans. by J.J. Doherty. Rev. ed. St. Louis, Herder, 1965, Chapters 105 (pp. 510-15) and 146 (pp. 665-69).

Murray, John Courtney, *Morality and Modern War*. New York, The Church Peace Union [now The Council on Religion and International Affairs], 1959. Also published as "Theology and Modern War." 10 *Theological Studies* (1959), 4061; in Nagle, *Morality and Modern Warfare, infra.,* pp. 69-91; in John Courtney Murray, *We Hold These Truths*. New York, Sheed & Ward, 1960; in Clancy, *Moral Dilemma of Nuclear Weapons, supra.,* pp. 7-16.

Murray, Thomas E., *Nuclear Policy for War and Peace*. Cleveland, World Publishing Company, 1960.

Nagle, William J. (ed.), *Morality and Modern Warfare*. Baltimore, Helicon, 1960.

Ramsey, Paul, *The Limits of Nuclear War: Thinking About the Do-Able and and the Un-Do-Able*. New York, The Council on Religion and International Affairs, 1963.

———— *War and the Christian Conscience*. Durham, Duke University Press, 1961.

Regout, Robert, *La doctrine de la guerre juste de saint Augustin a nos jours d'après les théologiens et les juristes canoniques*. Paris, Pedone, 1935.

Rommen, Heinrich A., *The State in Catholic Thought*. St. Louis, Herder, 1945, especially Ch. XXIX, "The Catholic Doctrine About War," pp. 641-71.

Ryan, John K., *Modern War and Basic Ethics*. Milwaukee, Bruce Publishing Co., 1940.

St. John-Stevas, Norman, *The Right to Life*. New York, Holt, Rinehart, and Winston, 1963, 1964.

Tucker, Robert W., *The Just War*. Baltimore, Johns Hopkins Press, 1960.

———— *Just War and Vatican Council II: A Critique*. New York, Council on Religion and International Affairs, 1966.

———— and Osgood, Robert, *Force, Order and Justice*. Baltimore, Johns Hopkins Press, 1967.

Vanderpol, Alfred, *La doctrine scolastique du droit de guerre*. Paris, Pedone, 1919.

B. *Articles and Periodicals*

Böckle, Franz, "Peace and Modern Warfare: Theological Discussion in Germany." *Concilium* 15: *War, Poverty, Freedom: A Christian Response,* ed. Franz Böckle. Glen Rock, N. J., Paulist Press, 1966, pp. 129-41.

Buzzard, Anthony, "The Christian Conscience and Modern War." *Worldview,* Vol. 7 (April, 1964), pp. 2-4.

Connery, John R., "Morality of Nuclear Armaments." *Theology Digest,* Vol. 5, no. 1 (Winter, 1957), pp. 9-12; republished in, Nagle, *Morality in Nuclear War, supra.,* pp. 92-7.

Conway, Edward A., "Pius XII on H-Bomb Tests." *Catholic Mind,* Vol. 55 (December, 1957), pp. 487-97.

──── "Review of Ideas on Just War: Vitoria and Suarez." *Catholic Messenger,* Vol. 81 (November, 1963), p. 2.

Delos, J.T., "The Sociology of Modern Warfare and the Theory of Just War." *Cross Currents,* Vol. 8 (Summer, 1958), pp. 248-66.

Dougherty, James E., "The Morality and Strategy of Deterrence." *The Catholic World,* Vol. 194 (March, 1962), pp. 337-44.

──── "The Catholic Church, War and Nuclear Weapons." *Orbis,* Vol. 9, no. 4 (Winter, 1966), pp. 845-97.

Enthoven, Alain, "Reason, Morality and Defense Policy." *America,* Vol. 108 (April 6, 1963), pp. 461-65; (April 13, 1963), pp. 494-97; (April 27, 1963), pp. 597-98.

Fleck, James C., "The Just War Theory — Past, Present, Future." *The Homiletic and Pastoral Review,* Vol. 67 (July, 1966), pp. 819-25; and "The Just War Theory — Past, Present, Future II: Positions, Principles." *The Homiletic and Pastoral Review,* Vol. 67 (August, 1966), pp. 905-18; comments on Father Fleck's article in pp. 912-18.

Ford, John C., "The Hydrogen Bombing of Cities." *Theology Digest,* Vol. 1 (Winter, 1957), pp. 6-9; republished in Nagle, *Morality and Nuclear Warfare, supra.,* pp. 98-103.

──── "The Morality of Obliteration Bombing." *Theological Studies,* Vol. 5 (September, 1944), pp. 261-309.

Gundlach, Gustav, "Die Lehre Pius XII zum Atomkrieg." *Stimmen der Zeit* (April, 1959), pp. 1-14. French translation, "Pie XII et la guerre atomique." *Documents,* Vol. 3 (May-June, 1959), pp. 268-84.

Hartigan, Richard S., "Non-Combatant Immunity: Its Scope and Development." *Continuum,* Vol. 3 (March, 1966), pp. 300-14.

Lefever, Ernest W., "The Just War Doctrine: Is It Relevant to the Nuclear Age?" *Worldview,* Vol. 4 (October, 1961), pp. 7-10.

McKenna, Joseph C., "Ethics and War: A Catholic View." *The American Political Science Review,* Vol. 54, no. 3 (September, 1960), pp. 647-58.

Ouwerkerk, Coenraad van, "Theological Discussion in Holland and France on Modern Warfare." *Concilium* 15: *War, Poverty, Free-*

dom: The Christian Response, ed. Franz Böckle. Glen Rock, N. J., Paulist Press, 1966, pp. 119-28.

Ramsey, Paul, "The Vatican Council on Modern War." *Theological Studies,* Vol. 27, no. 2 (June, 1966), pp. 179-203.

Theisen, Sylvester P., "Man and Nuclear Weapons." *The American Benedictine Review,* Vol. 14 (September, 1963), pp. 365-90.

Watkin, E.I., "Unjustifiable War." *Cross Currents,* Vol. 9 (Summer, 1959), pp. 225-32.

Zamayon, P., "Morality of War Today and In the Future." *Theology Digest,* Vol. 5 (Winter, 1957), pp. 2-5.

COLLECTIONS OF CHURCH DOCUMENTS AND COMMENTARIES THEREON

Flannery, Harry W. (ed.), *Pattern for Peace: Catholic Statements on International Order.* Westminster, Maryland, Newman Press, 1962.

The Pope Speaks. The American Quarterly of Papal Documents. Washington, D. C. 10 vols. to date.

PACIFIST LITERATURE ON MORALITY AND NUCLEAR WAR

A. Books

Anscombe, G.E.M. (ed.), *Nuclear Weapons: A Catholic Response.* New York, Sheed & Ward, 1962.

Bainton, Roland H., *Christian Attitudes toward War and Peace.* New York/Nashville, Abingdon Press, 1960.

King-Hall, Stephen, *Defense in the Nuclear Age.* Nyack, New York, Fellowship Publications, 1959.

Lawler, Justus George, *Nuclear War, The Ethic, The Rhetoric, The Reality.* Westminster, Maryland, Newman Press, 1965.

Merton, Thomas, *Original Child Bomb.* New York, New Directions, 1962.

Stein, Walter (ed.), *Nuclear Weapons and Christian Conscience.* London, Merlin Press, 1961.

Stratmann, Franziskus, *War and Christianity Today.*

Thompson, Charles S. (ed.), *Morals and Missiles: Catholic Essays on the Problem of War Today.* London, J. Clarke, 1959.

Tooke, Joan B., *The Just War in Aquinas and Grotius.* London, SPCK, 1965.

Toynbee, Philip (ed.), *The Fearful Choice*. Detroit, Wayne State University Press, 1959.

Zahn, Gordon, *An Alternative to War*. New York, The Council on Religion and International Affairs, 1963.

B. *Articles and Periodicals*

Dewart, Leslie, "War and the Christian Conscience." *Commonweal*, vol. 77 (November 2, 1962), pp. 145-48.

Douglass, James W., "The Morality of Thermonuclear Deterrence." *Worldview*, vol. 7 (October, 1964), pp. 4-8.

———— "Nuclear Morality and Eschatological Realism." *The Catholic World*, vol. 198 (December, 1963), pp. 177-84.

———— "Peace and the Overkill Strategists." *Cross Currents*, vol. 14 (Winter, 1964), pp. 87-103.

Griffiths, B., "Non-Violence and Nuclear War." *The Catholic Worker*, vol. 27 (June, 1961), p. 1.

Lawler, Justus George, "The Council Must Speak," and "Moral Issues and Nuclear Pacifism." *Peace, The Churches, and The Bomb*, ed. James Finn. New York, The Council on Religion and International Affairs, 1965.

Merton, Thomas, "Christian Ethics and Nuclear War." *The Catholic Worker*, vol. 28 (March and April, 1962), p. 1.

———— "Nuclear War and Christian Responsibility." *Commonweal*, vol. 75 (February 9, 1962), pp. 509-13.

———— "An Open Letter to the American Hierarchy." *Worldview*, vol. 8 (September, 1965), pp. 4-7.

Stein, Walter, "Would You Press the Button?" and "Limits of Nuclear War: Is A Just Deterrence Strategy Possible?" *Peace, The Churches, and The Bomb*, ed. James Finn. New York, Council on Religion and International Affairs, 1965.

Westow, Theodore L., "The Argument About Pacifism: A Critical Survey of English Studies." Concilium 15: *War, Poverty, Freedom: A Christian Response*, ed. Franz Böckle. Glen Rock, N. J., Paulist Press, 1966, pp. 105-18.

ARMS CONTROL AND DISARMAMENT; NATIONAL SECURITY POLICY

Arms Control and Disarmament: A Quarterly Bibliography with Abstracts and Annotations. Published by the United States Arms Control and Disarmament Agency.

Barker, Charles A. (ed.), *Problems of World Disarmament: A Series of Lectures Delivered at The Johns Hopkins University.* Boston, Houghton Mifflin, 1963.

Bechhoefer, Bernhard, *Postwar Negotiations for Arms Control.* Washington, The Brookings Institution, 1961.

Berkowitz, Morton and Bock, P.G. (eds.), *American National Strategy: A Reader in Theory and Policy.* New York, The Free Press, 1965.

Birrenbach, Kurt, *The Future of the Atlantic Community: Toward European-American Partnership.* New York, Praeger, 1963.

Boulding, Kenneth E., *Conflict and Defense: A General Theory.* New York, Harper and Row, 1962.

Brennan, Donald G., *Arms Control, Disarmament and National Security.* New York, George Braziller, 1961.

Brodie, Bernard, *Strategy in the Missile Age.* Princeton, Princeton University Press, 1959.

Bull, Hedley, *The Control of the Arms Race, Disarmament and Arms Control in the Missile Age.* Second edition. New York, Praeger, 1965.

Clausewitz, Carl von, *On War,* trans. by J.J. Graham. vol. II, Rev. ed. London, Routledge and Kegan Paul, 1962.

Clemens, Walter C., *World Perspectives on International Politics.* Boston, Little, Brown, 1965.

Cottrell, Alvin J. and Dougherty, James E., *The Politics of the Atlantic Alliance.* New York, Praeger, 1964.

Current Disarmament Proposals, As of March 1, 1964. Preliminary Edition. New York, World Law Fund, 1964. McVitty, Marion H. *A Comparison and Evaluation of Current Disarmament Proposals As of March 1, 1964.* New York, World Law Fund, 1964.

Dougherty, James E. and Lehman, John F., Jr. (eds.), *The Prospects for Arms Control.* New York, McFadden, 1965.

Gilpin, Robert, *American Scientists and Nuclear Weapons Policy.* Princeton, Princeton University Press, 1962.

Goldwin, Robert A. (ed.), *America Armed: Essays on United States Military Policy.* Chicago, Rand McNally, 1963.

Halperin, Morton H., *Limited War in the Nuclear Age.* New York, John Wiley, 1963.

Herz, John J., *International Politics in the Atomic Age.* New York, Columbia University Press, 1959.

Herzog, Arthur, *The War-Peace Establishment.* New York, Harper and Row, 1965.

Intercom., "Focus on Arms Control and Disarmament." Vol. 5, no. 2 (February-March, 1963).

Jacobson, H. K. and Stein, Eric, *Diplomats, Scientists and Politicians: The United States and the Nuclear Test-Ban Negotiations.* Ann Arbor, University of Michigan Press, 1966.

Kahn, Herman, *On Escalation: Metaphors and Scenarios.* New York, Praeger, 1965.

———— *On Thermonuclear War.* Second edition. Princeton, Princeton University Press, 1961.

———— *Thinking About the Unthinkable.* London, Weidenfeld and Nicolson, 1962.

Kaufmann, William W., *The McNamara Strategy.* New York, Harper and Row, 1964.

Kissinger, Henry A. (ed.), *Problems of National Strategy.* New York, Praeger, 1965.

Lall, Arthur S., *Negotiating Disarmament: The Eighteen Nation Disarmament Conference: The First Two Years, 1962-1964.* Ithaca, New York, Cornell University Center for International Studies, 1964.

Lall, Betty Goetz, *Nuclear Weapons: Can Their Spread Be Halted?* New York, The Council on Religion and International Affairs, 1965.

Lefever, Ernest W., *Arms and Arms Control.* New York, Praeger, 1962.

Levine, Robert A., *The Arms Debate.* Cambridge, Havard University Press, 1963.

McClelland, Charles A. (ed.), *Nuclear Weapons, Missiles and Future War.* San Francisco, Chandler Publishing Co., 1960.

National Citizens Commission on Arms Control and Disarmament. *Report* prepared for the White House Conference on International Cooperation, November 29-December 1, 1965. New York, United Nations Association of the United States of America, 1965. (Copies available from The Disarmament Issues Committee of UNA-USA, 345 West 46th Street, New York, New York 10017.

Osgood, Robert, *Limited War.* Chicago, University of Chicago Press, 1957.

Rabinowitch, Eugene, *The Dawn of a New Age: Reflections on Science and Human Affairs.* Chicago, University of Chicago Press, 1963.

Rapoport, Anatol, *Strategy and Conscience.* New York, Harper and Row, 1964.

Schelling, Thomas C., *The Strategy of Conflict.* New York, Oxford University Press, 1963.

———— *Arms and Influence.* New Haven & London, Yale University Press, 1966.

———— and Halperin, Morton H., *Strategy and Arms Control.* New York, The Twentieth Century Fund, 1961.

United States Arms Control and Disarmament Agency, *Documents on Disarmament 1945-1964.* 7 vols. Washington, Government Printing Office, 1960-1964.

———— *Synopses of Research Projects on Arms Control and Disarma-*

ment Sponsored by the U.S. Arms Control and Disarmament Agency Through August, 1965. Washington, U.S. Arms Control and Disarmament Agency, 1965.

———— *To Prevent the Spread of Nuclear Weapons.* USACDA publication 26. Washington, Government Printing Office, 1965.

United States Department of Defense, Office, Deputy Assistant Secretary, Arms Control, Office Assistant Secretary, International Security Affairs, *U.S. Security, Arms Control, and Disarmament. 1961-1965.* Washington, Department of Defense, 1965.

———— Special Assistant to the Joint Chiefs of Staff for Disarmament Affairs. *Disarmament: A Bibliographic Record, 1916-1960.* Prepared by the Staff of the Army Library. Washington, Government Printing Office, 1960.

United States Department of State, External Research Staff, *Arms Control and Disarmament: Studies in Progress or Recently Completed, 1963.* Washington, Bureau of Intelligence and Research, Department of State, 1963.

———— *Arms Control and Disarmament: Studies in Progress or Recently Completed, November 1964.*

Waskow, Arthur I., *Keeping the World Disarmed.* Santa Barbara, Center for the Study of Democratic Institutions, 1965.

INTERNATIONAL RELATIONS THEORY: INTERNATIONAL LAW, ORGANIZATION AND MORALITY

Aron, Raymond, *Paix et Guerre entre les nations.* Paris, Calman-Levy, 1962.

Bosc, Robert, *La société internationale et l'Eglise.* Paris, Editions SPES, 1961.

———— *Sociologie de la Paix.* Paris, Editions SPES, 1965.

Brandon, Donald, *American Foreign Policy, Beyond Utopianism and Realism.* New York, Appleton-Century-Crofts, 1966.

Claude, Inis, *Power and International Relations.* New York, Random House, 1962.

———— *Swords Into Plowshares.* Third edition. New York, Random House, 1964.

Falk, Richard A. and Mendlovitz, Saul H. (eds.), *The Strategy of World Order.* 4 vols. New York, World Law Fund, 1966.

Geyer, Alan F., *Piety and Politics: American Protestantism in the World Arena.* Richmond, Virginia, John Knox Press, 1963.

Halperin, Morton H., *Contemporary Military Strategy.* Boston, Little, Brown, 1965.

Herz, John H., *Political Realism and Political Idealism*. Chicago, University of Chicago Press, 1951.

Hilsman, Roger and Good, Robert C. *Foreign Policy in the Sixties*. Baltimore, The Johns Hopkins Press, 1965.

Hoffmann, Stanley (ed.), *Contemporary Theory in International Relations*. Englewood Cliffs, New Jersey, Prentice-Hall, 1960.

———— *The State of War: Essays in the Theory and Practice of International Politics*. New York, Praeger, 1965.

Lefever, Ernest W., *Ethics and United States Foreign Policy* New York, Meridian Books, 1957, 1959.

———— (ed.), *The World Crisis and American Responsibility: Nine Essays by Reinhold Niebuhr*. New York, Association Press, 1958.

McDougal, Myres S. and Feliciano, Florentino P., *Law and Minimum World Public Order: The Legal Regulation of International Coercion*. New Haven, Yale University Press, 1961.

O'Brien, William, "Legitimate Military Necessity in Nuclear War." *World Polity*, Vol. 2 (1960), pp. 35-120.

Osgood, Robert, *Ideals and Self-Interest in America's Foreign Relations*. Chicago, University of Chicago Press, 1953.

Sora, Alfred de, *International Morality*, trans. by S.J. Tester. New York, Hawthorn Books, 1963.

Thompson, Kenneth W., *Political Realism and the Crisis of World Politics*. Princeton, Princeton University Press, 1960.

Worldview. Published nine times a year by the Council on Religion and International Affairs. 9 vols. to date. 1958-1966.

COMMUNIST THOUGHT ON DEFENSE, ARMS CONTROL AND DISARMAMENT

Dallin, Alexander, and others, *The Soviet Union, Arms Control and Disarmament*. New York, Columbia University School of International Affairs, 1964.

H. S. Dinerstein, *War and the Soviet Union*, rev. ed. New York/London, Praeger, 1962.

Halperin, Morton H. and Perkins, Dwight H., *Communist China and Arms Control*. Cambridge, East Asian Research Center, Center for International Affairs, Harvard University, 1965.

United States Department of State, *Soviet World Outlook: A Handbook of Communist Statements*. Washington, Government Printing Office, 1959.

Wolfe, Thomas W., *Soviet Strategy at the Crossroads*. Cambridge, Harvard University Press, 1964.

CUBAN MISSILE CRISIS, 1962

Abel, Elie, *The Missile Crisis*. New York, J.P. Lippincott, 1966.
Larson, David L., *The Cuban Crisis of 1962, Selected Documents and Chronology*. Boston, Houghton Mifflin, 1963.

HIROSHIMA AND NAGASAKI

Alperovitz, Gar, *Atomic Diplomacy: Hiroshima and Potsdam*. New York, Simon and Schuster, 1965.
Amrine, Michael, *The Great Decision*. New York, Putnam, 1959.
Batchhelder, Robert, *The Irreversible Decision*. New York, Macmillan, 1965.
Fogelman, Edwin, *Hiroshima: The Decision to Use the A-Bomb*. New York, Scribner's, 1964.
Giovannitti, Len and Freed, Fred, *The Decision to Drop the Bomb*. New York, Coward-McCann, 1965.
Hersey, John, *Hiroshima*. New York, Bantam Books, 1946.

EFFECTS OF NUCLEAR EXPLOSIONS

Glasstone, Samuel (ed.), *The Effects of Nuclear Weapons*. Rev. ed. prepared by the U.S. Department of Defense; published by the U.S. Atomic Energy Commission. Washington, Government Printing Office, 1962.
Heer, David M., *After Nuclear Attack: a Demographic Inquiry*. New York-Washington-London, Praeger, 1965.
Stonier, Tom, *Nuclear Disaster*. Cleveland, Meridian Books, 1964.
United States House of Representatives, Subcommittee on Department of Defense Appropriations, Committee on Appropriations, *Hearings of Defense Appropriations for 1966*, part. 3. 89th Cong., 1st Sess. Washington, Government Printing Office, 1965.